50 ARCHITECTS 50 BUILDINGS

The buildings that inspire architects

First published in the United Kingdom in 2016 by
Batsford
1 Gower Street
London
WC1E 6HD

An imprint of Pavilion Books Group Ltd

ISBN: 9781849943420

A CIP catalogue record for this book is available from the British Library.

10 9 8 7 6 5 4 3 2 1

Repro by ColourDepth, UK
Printed by 1010 Printing International Ltd, China

This book can be ordered direct from the publisher at the website:

www.pavilionbooks.com, or try your local bookshop.

This book is published in association with the Twentieth Century Society,
which campaigns to safeguard the heritage of architecture and design in
Britain from 1914 onwards. It is a charity and a membership organisation,
with an official role in the planning process in England. A prime objective
is to extend the understanding and appreciation of buildings of our
period, and thereby facilitate their conservation. Join the Society at
www.c20society.org.uk/join/

50 Architects 50 Buildings brings together a selection of articles on
twentieth century buildings first published in the architecture newspaper
Building Design as part of its Inspiration series, which ran in print from
2009–2014 and has since continued online. BD is the leading online
source of news, comment and building, book and exhibition reviews
keeping architects up to date with the key issues affecting the practice
and profession of architecture. It includes a lively comment section
where the profession debates the issues raised by these stories. BD also
publishes the WA100 ranking of the world's top architectural practices
and runs the highly respected BD Architect of the Year Awards.

50 ARCHITECTS 50 BUILDINGS

The buildings that inspire architects

Edited by Pamela Buxton

Photographs by Gareth Gardner and Edward Tyler

BATSFORD

Introduction 6

The Architects 8

Introduction

Buildings that inspire architects

How do architects get their ideas? How do they learn from other people's buildings to make their own work richer and more satisfying? Architects draw on all sorts of amazing sources, including music, fine art, numbers and nature, but all architects visit other people's buildings, whether as a deliberate act of pilgrimage, a fact-finding mission or, inescapably, in the course of day-to-day life. For many architects, one building stands out as having had a transformative and long-term impact on their own designs. In this book architects share these often life-changing encounters with other architects' amazing buildings.

Pamela Buxton had the very enviable job of taking fifty of the most interesting architects working in Britain today to visit the buildings which have inspired them most. Commissioned by the architectural publication *Building Design*, the records of these trips by Pamela and photographers Gareth Gardner and Edward Tyler capture the experience of each visit, and are brought together here as a collection for the first time. Together they encourage us to see these inspirational buildings afresh through an architect's eyes, and understand why it was that these buildings made such an impression on them.

What does inspire mean?

"Inspire" was an important choice of word: the participants were not asked to pick their favourite building, or to attempt to select a "best" building – indeed sometimes difficult and flawed buildings are more inspiring than perfect ones. To inspire means to fill someone with the urge or ability to do or feel something, especially to do something creative. Some participants describe their choices as "profoundly moving" or feeling "like coming home" – the sort of analogies we draw when talking about finding a human soul mate. Although they could have taken *Building Design* to gothic cathedrals or baroque palaces, the majority looked back no further than the beginning of the last century, and picked C20 buildings. The architecture of the C20, and modernism in particular, seems to be what excites today's architects most.

First encounters

What is the first building you can remember being in? Many of our earliest memories are of places and the emotions they provoked. I'm struck by the fact that many of the architects here choose buildings they have known for an extremely long time and, not surprisingly, many initially encountered the buildings they selected in architectural books and magazines, and first visited them themselves as students, sometimes returning again and again over subsequent years. But some go even further back. James Soane picks the Liverpool Playhouse Extension; not a very famous building, but one to which he feels an intensely autobiographical relationship. Not only was it "conceived" in the same

year as he was, but his father was its engineer, and had a picture of it over his desk. James recalls how "it entered into my consciousness before I even knew what architecture was" and "made me aware of modern architecture before I knew anything about it".

Another native Liverpudlian, Paul Monaghan, picks Liverpool's Roman Catholic Cathedral, "Paddy's Wigwam"– a building he admires because it is "really loved by the public", and is where his whole school went for services. Niall McLaughlin chooses "the building that made me want to be an architect", ABK's Trinity College Dublin Library, and he recounts how he was all set to study English at university until he looked carefully at this building, and its "extraordinary vividness" had such an impact on him that he changed to study architecture.

Many architects are enthusiastic travellers, and young architects often take work abroad, sometimes for their "year out" – the year (or more) spent working in architects' offices between undergraduate and post graduate study – architectural education is a long haul. Many of the buildings selected here were first seen at this point, and some of our architects had personal encounters with their heroes. Edward Jones first went to Eliel Saarinen's Cranbrook campus to take life-drawing classes when he was working for Eliel's son Eero for a summer – that must have led to some interesting conversations. Chris Williamson had a spell working in New York, and then headed west to California where in 1980 he could wander into the garden of the Eames House and find Ray Eames still living and working there. Some of the first encounters were casual or even illicit (there's some squeezing though hoardings, and climbing over locked gates recalled here). But some architects had very formal introductions: Michál Cohen went to the newly completed Hellerup School on a British Council study trip and was shown round by the head teacher. Some architects went alone, some with their colleagues, some added on a visit as a treat after teaching in a new city, or visiting a site for a forthcoming project. I suspect the itineraries of some family holidays were tweaked to take in a special place, somewhere long lodged in the subconscious or freshly spotted in a journal.

Revisiting

All these circumstances and more impact on how a place affects us, and going back with Pamela and a photographer specifically for this project was always going to be a different experience. Many participants reflect on these differences, and how they and the places have changed. Some first visits were made when buildings were brand new architecture, some have now shifted status to be regarded as historic buildings. Sometimes the original use has weathered this change; sometimes buildings now have a very different role. There are buildings that have decayed while others have been spruced up and restored. Some architects are uneasy about over-restoration, some would love to get the job of sweeping away disfiguring accretions, or sorting out those little bits that in their opinion never worked in the first place. Perhaps most surprisingly Jon Buck and Dominic Cullinan chose somewhere they had never actually been before, and made their first ever trip to Leicester Engineering Building. Might it have inspired them differently if they had actually visited earlier?

How do buildings inspire architects?

The hardest question these encounters raise is exactly how these buildings have inspired the architects who have selected them. Some of them talk directly about this: Sean Griffiths is provocatively flippant when he tells us that "FAT has nicked many ideas [from Loos' American Bar]". Jonathan Ellis-Miller is now amused at "how blindingly obvious" the influence of Hopkins has been on his firm's work "in terms of plan, aesthetic and organisation of space." There is a bit a self-deprecation there, but also an innate self confidence that each has added something extra and created something new. In contrast, Tony Fretton is adamant that he can't see any Asplund influences in his own work. And, of course, architects and critics can have different interpretations of what is going on. Sometimes we remain so close to something we have created ourselves that we can't see it remotely objectively.

Building an inner library

The late Jonathan Woolf went to see the Krefeld Villas to study brickwork for a commission where he chose to use brick for the first time, but few of these buildings have been so consciously picked out for individual project research. I like Tim Ronalds' reflection that he returns to Gothenburg Law Courts "not so much to copy ideas or forms directly, rather to recharge my aspirations". Others talk of a specific buildings as a "touchstone", "a reference", "a pin-up for us" or "as a starting point". "Borrowings", of whatever form, may be recognised and acknowledged at the time, or only realised much later. Biba Dow says she can only now "see subliminal analogies" between her choice of inspirational building and the practice's own work. Marie-José van Hee talks about how a building "goes right into your inner map, your personal library, and you never know when and how it will come out again until it does."

Working as part of a team, architects, generally unfairly, get a reputation for arrogance. Here they reveal both longings and vulnerability. Sole practitioner Niall McLaughlin, reflecting on ABK, the architects of his chosen building, envies the camaraderie of having soul mates to work with, and rather than selecting buildings where a single architect is seen as a lone creative genius. Many participants choose buildings which exemplify the importance of a good working relationship with an inspiring client – sometimes with a bit of wistful envy!

Confounding expectations

What I particularly like about all the stories told here is that they make the point that actually visiting a building is a very different experience to reading about it, seeing photos, or even watching a film or digital modelling. Sometimes a visit confounds our expectations. I, too, have found that a building I thought I knew well from photos was in a totally different location to the one I was expecting, or unexpectedly "dinky" or "something you can cuddle rather than something that overawes you" as Cullinan and Buck say of the Leicester Engineering Building. Visiting a building allows you to soak up the atmosphere of a place, the sounds and shadows, the feel of rough board-marked concrete, the breeze from a half open window, the reflections on the ceiling from the pool outside. By visiting you can observe the patterns people make as they use the space, where they like to sit, how they work out where to go, how the building makes them behave and feel. It's because this can never be fully captured nor replicated that C20 Society campaigns to keep real, actual buildings on the sites where they were constructed. It's also why we like to take people to see buildings for real too. Like the architects here, some of our members are designers or knowledgeable historians too. When we visit buildings in a group, knowing details of how projects came about is important to some, others just want to bathe in an intense atmosphere, or imagine the essence of a building seeping into them. Some want to sketch or photograph, like these architects, to record, understand or explore.

Challenges to our perceptions, as well as the confirmation of anticipated delight, are what visiting great architecture is all about. We hope you will enjoy being an armchair visitor with these architects, and be inspired to make your own visits too.

Catherine Croft
Director of the C20 Society

As well as campaigning for the preservation of architecture in the UK from 1914 onwards, the C20 Society organises trips in Britain and abroad. Find out more and join online.

www.C20society.org.uk

The Architects

David Archer is co-founder of Archer Humphryes Architects, which specialises in the design of hotels, restaurants, residences and resorts. Notable work includes Chiltern Firehouse and Great Northern Hotel in London, as well as Hakkasan and Busaba Eathai for restaurateur and long-standing client Alan Yau.

Cany Ash is a founder partner of Ash Sakula Architects. The practice works extensively in the arts, education and housing sectors with key projects including the UK Centre for Carnival Arts in Luton, Peabody housing in Silvertown and the Hothouse arts centre in Hackney, London.

Peter Barber has run his own practice since 1989, specialising mainly in mixed-use and residential regeneration schemes. Key London projects include the Donnybrook Quarter in Bow, the Spring Gardens homeless accommodation in Hither Green and the Employment Academy in Camberwell.

Rab and Denise Bennetts established Bennetts Associates in London in 1987 followed by the addition of an Edinburgh office in 1994. Since then the practice has steadily grown to around 85 people with projects including the redesign of the Royal Shakespeare Theatre in Stratford.

Michál Cohen was born in South Africa, studied architecture in KwaZulu Natal and London and set up Walters & Cohen Architects with Cindy Walters in 1994. Through research and in practice, she has developed a strong interest in the link between the design of education buildings and learning.

Tom Coward is an architect and director of AOC. Based in East London, the practice aims to design generous architecture that is both beautiful and socially engaged. Diverse projects include a Reading Room for the Wellcome Collection, the Spa secondary school in London's Southwark and The Green, a community centre in south London.

Ted Cullinan is the founder of Cullinan Studio. He has designed more than 110 buildings including the Grade II* listed Ready Mix Concrete Headquarters in Egham and the Weald and Downland Gridshell in West Sussex. He is the recipient of many top accolades including the RIBA Gold Medal in 2008.

Biba Dow and **Alun Jones** formed Dow Jones Architects in 2000. The practice works across private, public and commercial sectors, with key projects including a Maggie's Centre in Cardiff, refurbishment of Christ Church Spitalfields crypt, and The Garden Museum, both in London.

Jonathan Ellis-Miller, a London based architect and teacher, set up EllisMiller Architects in 1991. He has been responsible for designing notable projects including Mansell Street in the City of London, the Catmose education and community campus in Oakham and the Women's Institute HQ in Cambridge.

Alex Ely is an architect, planner and founder of Mæ architects. As well as designing a wide range of housing and urban design he was the author of the Mayor of London's Housing Design Guide and has contributed to publications for the Commission for Architecture and the Built Environment.

Sarah Featherstone is an architect and director of Featherstone Young, a practice working in the housing, community, cultural and education sectors. She teaches at Central Saint Martins and is a Civic Trust Award assessor and a Design Review panellist for several local authorities.

Tony Fretton has been in practice since 1982, designing a wide range of cultural, public, residential and office buildings with an emphasis on creating a sense of place. Key projects include the British Embassy in Warsaw (2009), the Red House in Chelsea (2001) and the Lisson Gallery (1990), also in London.

Cuban-born **Edgar Gonzalez** is a co-founder of London-based practice Brisac Gonzalez. Key projects include the Museum of World Culture in Gothenburg, Le Prisme Concert Hall in Aurillac, and The Pajol Sports Centre in Paris. Ongoing work includes a 18,000m² mixed-use scheme in Paris.

Piers Gough is an architect, writer and co-founder of the award-winning architectural practice CZWG. His best known work includes the Canada Water Library in Rotherhithe, the Green Bridge in Mile End, East London, and the Maggie's Cancer Care Centre in Nottingham.

Tom Grieve and Hana Loftus are co-founders of Colchester-based architects HAT Projects. Work includes the Jerwood Gallery in Hastings, High House Artists' Studios in Purfleet, Essex, and Gasworks arts complex in London. HAT Projects was RIBA East Emerging Architect of the Year 2014.

Sean Griffiths was a founder member of the architecture studio Fashion Architecture Taste (FAT), whose work included A House for Essex designed with artist Grayson Perry and Islington Square housing in Manchester. He is Professor of Architecture at the University of Westminster in London.

Roger Hawkins and **Russell Brown** set up Hawkins\Brown in 1988. The practice works across the education, residential, transport, commercial, cultural and civic sectors. Projects include three Crossrail stations, the Corby Cube civic centre and the regeneration of the Park Hill estate in Sheffield.

Graham Haworth is co-founder of Haworth Tompkins, a practice with a particular expertise in the cultural, education and housing sectors. Recent projects include the Royal College of Art's Dyson Building in Battersea, and the regeneration of the National Theatre on London's South Bank.

Stephen Hodder is founder of Manchester-based architects Hodder + Partners and a past president of the Royal Institute of British Architects. His practice was the inaugural winner of the prestigious Stirling Prize in 1996 for the Centenary Building at the University of Salford.

Simon Hudspith is a founding partner of Panter Hudspith Architects, and has extensive experience designing buildings in historic settings as well as mixed-use, residential and cultural buildings. He is also a national panel member for CABE, the Southwark Design Review Panel and Design South East.

Edward Jones is co-founder with Jeremy Dixon of Dixon Jones, architects of the Royal Opera House, the National Portrait Gallery, and the re-design of Exhibition Road in London. The practice also designed Kings Place in Kings Cross, and the Said Business School at Oxford University.

Adam Khan designs public buildings, social housing and private houses in both the UK and overseas. Notable projects include the £22million regeneration of a Danish housing estate and the competition-winning design for the Brockholes Visitor Centre in Lancashire, which created a cluster of buildings floating on a large pontoon.

David Kohn is director of David Kohn Architects (DKA). He studied architecture at the University of Cambridge and Columbia University, New York. DKA's work includes A Room for London, a one-room installation in the form of a boat created with artist Fiona Banner on the roof of the Queen Elizabeth Hall on London's Southbank.

Julian Lewis is a director of architectural and urban design practice East. He is visiting critic to the Mayor's Design Advisory Group, and a member of the Newham Design Review Panel. East focuses on projects of public relevance including housing, schools, community buildings and public spaces.

MJ Long, the widow and former professional partner of British Library architect Colin St.John Wilson, is a partner at Long & Kentish. The practice has a particular specialism in libraries and also designs galleries, museums and studios. MJ Long has taught at Yale School of Architecture in Connecticut since 1973.

Patrick Lynch established Lynch Architects in 1998 in London. Recent London work includes the Kings Gate apartments on Victoria Street, The National Youth Theatre in North London and a library in Westminster. Marsh View, a holiday house for an artist, was exhibited at the Venice Biennale in 2012.

Gerard Maccreanor is co-founder with Richard Lavington of Maccreanor Lavington. The UK and Netherlands-based practice has won 42 architectural awards including six RIBA National Awards and the Stirling Prize, won in 2008 for the Accordia housing in Cambridge.

Educated in Dublin, **Niall McLaughlin** has run his own architecture practice in London since 1990. The practice works broadly across a variety of building types, with recent award-winning projects including the Bishop Edward King Chapel and student residences for Somerville College, both in Oxford.

Paul Monaghan is a founding director of Allford Hall Monaghan Morris. Key projects include the BBC Television Centre master plan and the new Scotland Yard headquarters for the Metropolitan Police in Whitehall, central London. AHMM won the 2015 Stirling Prize for Burntwood School in South London.

Alex Mowat is an architect and founder of Mowat & Company (previously Urban Salon), which designs across the retail, museum, office, housing and education sectors. Clients include Peabody housing association, National Gallery, Victoria and Albert Museum, Design Museum and BRE.

Eric Parry established Eric Parry Architects in 1983, and has combined his practice with teaching, most notably at the University of Cambridge. Key projects include the renewal of St Martin-in-the-Fields Church in Trafalgar Square and the award-winning extension of the Holburne Museum of Art in Bath.

Greg Penoyre is co-founder and senior partner at Penoyre & Prasad, where he has played an important role in more than 300 projects across commercial and public sectors. Key buildings include the Ludwig Guttman Centre for Health and Well Being in Stratford and Swiss Cottage Special School, London.

RCKa was formed in 2008 by Tim Riley, Russell Curtis and Dieter Kleiner. The practice's aim is to produce vibrant, socially responsive buildings and places that support use and activity, encourage social interaction and cohesive communities, and are meaningful to the people that use them.

Richard Rogers is a founding partner of Rogers Stirk Harbour + Partners. In a career spanning more than fifty years, he and his partners have designed many buildings including Centre Pompidou, Lloyd's of London, the Welsh Assembly, the Millennium Dome and the Leadenhall Building in London.

Tim Ronalds is founder of Tim Ronalds Architects, which specialises in the design of arts, education and public buildings. Major projects include the regeneration of the Hackney Empire theatre and Ironmonger Row Baths, both in London, and the design of the Landmark Theatre in Ifracombe.

Peter St John is a partner of Caruso St John Architects, a practice with an international reputation for the design of public building projects, museums and galleries. The practice designed the New Art Gallery Walsall (2000), Tate Millbank Project (2014), and renovated and extended Stockholm City Library.

Dominic Cullinan and **Jon Buck** co-founded SCABAL (St Cullinan And Buck Architects Ltd) in 1997. Key projects include the Trumans Road Houses, Dunraven School Container Sports Hall and the Christ Church Spitalfields Nursery. Ongoing work includes education projects in India and London.

Takero Shimazaki is a director of London-based studio Takero Shimazaki Architects (formerly Toh Shimazaki Architecture). Works include OSh House, Centre For Sight, Curzon Bloomsbury and Leicester Print Workshop, each engaging deeply with context, history and materiality of sites.

James Soane is a founding partner of Project Orange, a research-led design practice, currently working on large-scale residential projects in the UK, hotels in India and an office building in Moscow. James is also Director of Critical Practice at the recently launched London School of Architecture.

Michael Squire founded Squire and Partners in 1976. Residential, office and masterplanning projects include apartment schemes One Tower Bridge and Clarges Mayfair, the Bulgari Hotel & Residences in Knightsbridge and the mixed-use One The Elephant development at Elephant & Castle.

Studio Egret West was founded by Christophe Egret and David West in 2004. The practice works widely across the housing, education, culture, health, public realm and mixed-use sectors. Notable projects include Clapham Library in south London and the regeneration of the Park Hill estate in Sheffield.

John Tuomey is co-founder with Sheila O'Donnell of Dublin-based practice O'Donnell + Tuomey, recipients of the Royal Gold Medal architecture prize in 2015. The practice has an expertise in cultural, social and educational buildings, with key projects including the Lyric Theatre in Belfast.

Hans van der Heijden is an architect living and working in Amsterdam and an editor of the Dutch Architecture Yearbook. He has been a professor in sustainable urban design at Cambridge University and was founder and creative director of Rotterdam architects biq from 1994–2014 before setting up his own practice.

Marie-José van Hee has run an architecture studio in Ghent, Belgium, since 1975. Her award-winning practice concentrates on public buildings, private houses and urban development with a focus on creating timeless architecture that offers a high quality of life. She also teaches extensively.

Keith Williams is the founder and director of Keith Williams Architects, a firm with a specialism in museum, gallery, library, music and performing arts buildings. Recent work includes Marlowe Theatre in Canterbury, the Novium Museum in Chichester and the National Opera House, Wexford.

Paul Williams is a director of Stanton Williams, winners of the Stirling Prize for Architecture in 2012. Key projects include the University of Arts London campus at King's Cross, Compton Verney Art Gallery, the Sainsbury Laboratory, and the Eton Manor venue for the London 2012 Olympics.

Chris Williamson is founding partner of architects and urban designers Weston Williamson + Partners. The practice has a specialism in transport, designing the Paddington Crossrail Station and the Kuala Lumpur Metro. Current work includes design development for Crossrail 2.

Stephen Witherford and **William Mann** are two of the three co-founders of Witherford Watson Mann Architects, which won the 2013 Stirling Prize for the residential renovation of the ruined Astley Castle in Warwickshire. Other projects include a UK headquarters for Amnesty International.

Jonathan Woolf (1961 – 2015) founded Jonathan Woolf Architects in 1991. He completed more than 35 projects, including a number of multi-generational dwellings in London, most notably the award-winning Brick Leaf house in Hampstead, north London, and Lost Villa in Nairobi, Kenya.

Clare Wright is a partner at Wright & Wright Architects, which she co-founded in 1994 with Sandy Wright. Completed work includes the Women's Library in London and Hull Truck Theatre. She is working on new libraries for Magdalen and St John's Colleges in Oxford and on a revamp of London's Geffrye Museum.

Workplace

CHILEHAUS

Eric Parry at the Chilehaus, a brick tour-de-force constructed with about four million clinker bricks.

Chilehaus

Location: Hamburg, Germany
Architect: Fritz Höger, with artist Richard Kuöhl
Completed: 1922–24
Chosen by Eric Parry of Eric Parry Architects

Chilehaus captures an extraordinarily vital moment in German culture, part of the great flowering of expressionism. It was built just a few years after the end of the First World War but has this terrific sense of the optimism and renewal of the time that proved to be all too brief.

I spent my adolescence in Liverpool, like Hamburg, another great port city. My grandfather was a marine engineer for shipping lines trading with the Far East and on the dock road the prows of ships, overshadowing the great nineteenth-century wall, were messengers from a world beyond. Chilehaus has a potent sense of this spirit of mercantile voyaging which appeals to me still.

I had seen the contemporaneous publication of the building on its completion in *Wasmuths Monatshefte für Baukunst* of 1924 but visited it for the first time when we had an office trip to see Peter Latz's seminal landscape work in the Ruhr. I now know the city well and have visited Chilehaus many times.

Chilehaus was designed by Fritz Höger, who came from a building craftsman's background steeped in the Hanseatic tradition of brickwork, 'der Backsteinarchitektur', in which buildings both sacred and secular shared the humble module as foundation for extraordinary inventiveness. With Chilehaus this earthbound tradition meets, in spirit, the esoteric idealism of Bruno Taut's *Alpine Architecture* (1917) and Lyonel Feininger's crystalline imagery of the same period.

Chilehaus is a populist building housing the offices of dozens of firms but its origins lie in the tradition of the Kontorhaus – the merchant building that combined warehouse, offices

and living accommodation. The porosity of the ground-floor level with the central court, public passages and retail units, is in essence an urban-scaled version of this tradition.

Chilehaus is a vast single entity whose scale demands two entrances which are placed to the east and west side of the central public court. A public route passes under the building from north to south-sloping towards the docks, and is marked by two load-bearing brick arches each of which comes to rest on six massive concrete piers. The piers and soffits are in themselves masterpieces of their craft as are a series of finely detailed, Bay Keramik loggias around the curtilage of the building.

These crafted elements are testimony to the close collaboration of Höger and sculptor Richard Kuöhl. Kuöhl was born in 1880 and grew up in Meissen, traditionally the centre of German ceramic art. He studied in Dresden and came to Hamburg following the appointment of Fritz Schumacher as Oberbaudirektor – the head of city architecture and planning. Schumacher led the rebuilding of the merchant city, a quarter stigmatised by a cholera epidemic at the end of the nineteenth century.

The design of office buildings as places of work and contributors to the city is close to my heart and I find Chilehaus inspiring on many levels – it's a sophisticated urban response on a par with other great city buildings. At the time, it would have been seen as audacious and an incredible investment by Höger's client Henry Sloman in the future of Hamburg's mercantile world. It soon became one of the most emblematic images of the city.

It has a muscularity but also a responsiveness in its articulation. A certain courage was needed

to take on a 200m-long site and think on that scale. It was the biggest office building in Europe at that time, with multiple entrances and some 2,800 windows, yet it doesn't seem overbearing. Instead, it has this extraordinary uplifting exuberance culminating in the iconic moment at the 'prow' on Pumpen and Burchardstrasse. Mies did the same thing in glass with his Friedrichstrasse project in Berlin at exactly the same time. Here, however, we are firmly in the Hanseatic world and the architectural expression is unmistakable and particular.

Höger was creating an urban complex. It is very pragmatic and rational, but like Borromini's oratory of Saint Phillip Neri in Rome, things aren't quite symmetrical – long walls respond to the urban condition. Höger thinks in urban terms, addressing the square across the street even though that means the urban passage that leads through the building isn't centralised.

He clearly undertook the challenge of designing a 480m-long elevation by gauging the impact of the building at different distances. He created a unified stepped cornice to read at the city scale; the building is arranged to respond to the new surrounding urban plan, and then he created more than a dozen distinct 'episodes' at street level, many of which are memorable, like the beautiful curve along Pumpen.

Höger had an extraordinary ability to work a façade once he had established a structural logic for the type of building. His use of brick to articulate the design was very clever and is reminiscent of Gaudi in Barcelona. I have not designed many brick buildings but find myself frustrated by the banal wallpapering of the material. My choice of this building is in part to hold a mirror up to the limp tectonic and

material platitudes of today, not least in Hamburg.

The brickwork has a closely understood structure. Flat panels above and below windows are simple, while in prominent areas like the archway over-panels they are a riot of textural brick weaving. The wall surface is given stiffness and relief by triangular vertical piers rising from the double-height base to the underside of the cornice. These in turn have an inflection every seventh course to give a scaling between window and wall. So often art and architecture become disassociated and art is left as an afterthought but here architect and artist were in close dialogue, both helping to create a result greater than the sum of its parts.

Chilehaus today continues to work as it was intended. It is essentially a passively controlled environment with a clever services distribution system from an innovative basement structure. The internal finishes of the common areas are simple and dignified, and the external envelope should be good for centuries to come. Not many contemporary buildings can boast such urban sustainable and aesthetic credentials.

Chilehaus terminates in a distinctive ship's prow-like corner, a probable reference to the client's mercantile business.

BRICK ICON Chilehaus was built by the shipping magnate Henry B Sloman and named in reference to the saltpetre from Chile that had made his fortune. Sloman commissioned Fritz Höger to design the 10-storey building for Hamburg's then new merchant district, the first dedicated office zone in Europe.

Höger's design linked two irregularly shaped plots of land by building over the narrow Fischertwiete Street close to the River Elbe. The huge building is arranged around two internal courtyards to either side of this street, and terminates in a sharp corner reminiscent of a ship's prow at the intersection of Pumpen and Burchardstrasse. Chilehaus was built with more than 4 million dark clinker bricks on a reinforced concrete frame with sculptural elements by Richard Kuöhl.

Nearly a century later it retains most of its original features including its semi-public entrance halls. It is let to multiple office tenants with retail spaces and cafés at ground floor.

One of the two courtyards within the Chilehaus development. All elevations are lined in brick.

Above: One of the many entrances off the larger public courtyard. The building name refers to the client's business importing saltpetre from Chile.

Right: Chilehaus' semi-public entrance halls are lined in glazed ceramics. Eric Parry admires their "simple and dignified" quality.

Christophe Egret (left) and David West (right) of Studio
Egret West at the Zollverein Coal Mine Complex, which
now accommodates a variety of post-industrial uses.

Zollverein Coal Mine

Location: Essen, Germany
Architect: Martin Kremmer & Fritz Schupp
Built: 1927 (OMA-masterplanned regeneration from 2002)
Chosen by David West and Christophe Egret of Studio Egret West

David West

Zollverein has become a shorthand reference for us to explain to clients, communities and stakeholders a type of post-industrial environment that isn't sanitised through regeneration, but instead uses landscape and narrative to create a rich new platform for sustainable development. This creative re-use appeals to us because we enjoy the obstruction of retaining as much as possible and using resonance with the past to help discover new uses and place-specific designs.

Zollverein stands out for us not just through the nature and sheer ambition of the regeneration, but the quality of the original industrial architecture. You can see why it has been described as the most beautiful coal mine in the world. With its rigorously planned brick blocks, chimneys and chutes, it is designed to be absolutely utilitarian yet somehow the architecture becomes really playful and, when we visited, we all discovered something of the fairground about it.

Because it's such an unusual collection of buildings and spaces, Zollverein is good enough to have a second life, and this is an inspiration for any architect to make their buildings good enough for another incarnation. We admire the ambition and commitment that has sought this second role at Zollverein. Zollverein has the potential for this completely new layer of programme as a cultural and business centre on a monumental scale. Everything about it is extraordinary. The dramatic juxtaposition of new and old is very raw and strong. One of the key reasons that Zollverein has been such a pin-up for us at Studio Egret West is the untamed-yet-structured wilderness nature of the post-industrial landscape.

It's not too cosmetic or precious. Near the coal washery, the memory of the railway tracks is amplified when it would have been very easy to clear it all away. We like how the regeneration avoids clearing up the place to within an inch of its life. As a result, Zollverein retains a lot of its grit and specialness. So often architects overcomplicate things but this is a simple, pared-back restoration with one clear big move that brings it alive – the giant orange escalator up to the new museum, which adds a new, memorable element without dissolving the narrative of the past.

Zollverein has been an inspiration for us on many of the post-industrial landscapes we've worked on that have needed reinvention. We like to pull out stories from the site's history and show its layers, such as at the Old Vinyl Factory, the original home of HMV in Hayes.

So many developers take a corporate and banal route when creating what they think people want rather than concentrating on what differentiation a place can offer. There's no reason that business parks and offices have to be so dull. Why can't they be the inspirational working places of the future?

Reinvention does take time and at Zollverein they're taking a piece-by-piece approach to building out the masterplan including some memorable 'meanwhile' uses such as a 500m-long ice track and swimming pool at the coking plant which we like – our approach has always been that meanwhile is worthwhile. It's about slow-cooking change to gradually evolve a place, although because of the recession and the UNESCO restrictions the pace might have slowed down a little too much at Zollverein. There's a very long way to go, but at Zollverein, they're in it for the long haul.

Christophe Egret

This project has been one of our inspirations since we started our practice – a reinvention of disused, post-industrial heritage to create an active leisure park through a blend of urban design, inspired raw landscape, contemporary architecture and the reuse of old buildings.

A lot of architects are inspired by the architecture of individual buildings, but both David and I are particularly interested in the nature and architecture of a place as a whole, and on every site we work on we immerse ourselves to find the specificity of the site.

Zollverein is about sustainability. Here, industrial land is becoming a cultural landscape and it's a testimony to the place that it can evolve so well. This is inspiring for us because one of the important things for the future is adaptability.

It does go against the architect's ego and it is harder to adapt a building than design anew, but preserving rather than wiping the slate clean can be the catalyst for reinvention – if we keep that building, that tree, that landscape, we can keep a connection with the pulse of the place. Zollverein is a good example of this. None of the spaces are beautified. They still have a raw quality, apart perhaps from Foster's Red Dot museum. There must have been a time when it would have been quite attractive to demolish Zollverein but someone found the will to stick with it. Now the point has been made and it's a success.

Industrial architecture is interesting in that its shape does everything as efficiently as possible. Like a uniform, it's an aesthetic to do with function rather than fad. Zollverein

is dramatic but also harmonious and elegant. The approach of the regeneration has been to keep the soul of the past industry as an anchor for the creation of contemporary new uses. The danger, especially with the restrictions of its UNESCO status, was that it might have become a monument rather than a catalyst to regeneration.

What works so well is the meshing of the wild landscape with the tough, industrial environment. That for me is the magic moment. It draws the whole thing together and in our projects, we've always found that the one thing that really holds the spirit of the masterplan is the landscape – the paths, the streets, the squares.

When we visited, one of the most amazing parts was the room in the coking plant with the coal bunkers that resemble great concrete udders. You couldn't ever justify building something like that but because it's already there, you end up with a space that has so much more character than if the whole lot had just been swept away.

So many places that have been restored end up being sanitised — like the Fiat factory in Turin, which is now a mediocre shopping complex. Zollverein is full of resonance with the past. It just needs a bit more contemporary life, but that, I hope, will come.

Coal bunkers in the former coking plant. Many of Zollverein's industrial buildings have been utilised for site-specific art installations.

MINE REINVENTION Once the largest producing coal mine in the Ruhr area, Zollverein is now being regenerated as a mixed-use development. The mine, which covers 100ha in the north of Essen, was active from 1847 to 1986 with the coking plant operational from 1961–1993. The diverse site was rationalised to maximise productivity, with buildings arranged in strict symmetry in uniform red brick with steel frames.

The mine buildings were saved from demolition when it was decided to develop cultural and business uses for Zollverein. OMA's masterplan included the refurbishment of halls and open areas and the conversion of the coal-washing plant, the largest above-ground building, in 2003–6.

SANAA completed a new design school building in 2006 on the edge of the site, now occupied by Folkwang Academy. Foster & Partners' Red Dot design museum is housed in a former boiler-house. The whole site is a local recreation area and events venue. Zollverein became a UNESCO World Heritage Site in 2001.

Above (top): The former coal mine is now a recreation area, with several of the industrial buildings incorporating new mixed-uses such as museums and education.

Above (bottom): Many of the imposing 1920s red brick mine buildings are considered fine examples of Modern Movement architecture.

Above: New landscaping retains the spirit of the site's industrial past, incorporating many of the railway tracks that crossed the site.

Hana Loftus (left) and
Tom Grieve (right) of HAT
Projects at the Economist
Plaza in central London.

The Economist Plaza

Location: London, UK

Architects: Alison and Peter Smithson

Completed: 1959–64

Chosen by Tom Grieve and Hana Loftus of HAT Projects

Tom Grieve

I first encountered the Economist buildings as a child, scuttling across the plaza. So much of St James's is textured and rich, convulsing with decoration, and the thing that struck me was the unexpected cleanness and crisp sheen of the paving, and public spaces that were rich but severe, not dressed or carved.

In the middle of the city, pedestrian spaces felt luxurious and there was a sense of exhilaration at this perfect, empty space with no shopfronts or crowds. I had no understanding at all of the space, but having not had a very urban childhood, it was an experience that was part of my sense of London.

Long after this initial, purely sensory response, the Economist buildings became a place to understand as I learned to be an architect. Though widely celebrated, to me this building has always held a value from a purely experiential perspective. If I'm nearby I try to make a detour through the plaza, and I am always learning something new.

The way the buildings sit in the cityscape, and the experience from plaza and street level, are both beautifully crafted. The Smithsons put the smallest building of the three on to St James's Street, where it doesn't try to compete with the formality of the street itself. The highest volume abuts the narrow side street, where the perspective means that from ground level, you are almost unaware of its height. This successfully goes against those theories of massing which say that the wider streets should have the most imposing buildings or that these should 'hold the corner' and the massing of the other buildings step down from that. Yet it's so much more successful.

At ground level, the journey through the public spaces is a joyful exploration of stepping levels, oblique angles and many corners to look around. The project is incredibly generous in its contribution of public space. And of course, chopping the corners off the buildings to soften the edges is key, done in scale and proportion to both the buildings and the route you take around them.

The hierarchy of fenestration is managed very cleverly. The Smithsons manipulated the basic rhythm for different uses, with two-window bays for the Economist tower itself, wider, more horizontal proportions on the Bank tower, and on the residential building, single window, more vertical bays. We also look enviously at the quality of the materiality and detailing.

But the main reason I love these buildings is that they show that you don't have to be fearful when working in such sensitive locations. Here is a building that was built in the 1960s, in a part of London that is extremely establishment, with listed buildings coming out of its ears, yet right among it is this completely different building that does its job really well.

Fifty years on, as a culture we're still so tentative about working in these kinds of places. We don't seem to learn from the Smithsons' confidence in putting their ideas out there with no previous experience of building commercial development.

The Smithsons' work is radically inventive across a range of typologies, most of which they only built out in one iteration. What comes through in all of their projects is the importance, almost the deity, of public space. That's not about style or aesthetics – it's a point of principle.

Hana Loftus

My first experience of the building was when I was a student and I knew almost nothing about the Smithsons. The Economist buildings struck me as elegant in an almost foreign way. Solid rather than glassy, they made this wonderful, unusual public space that was intimate and yet strangely anonymous. The buildings held themselves at a slight remove without being recessive, just present, a part of the city.

The Smithsons were proper intellectuals, but the Economist scheme resists splashy statements in favour of a quiet subversion, based on a sophisticated and nuanced theory of urban development while responding to the history and accumulated meanings of its context. In the middle of this they felt able to make something with no overt reference to any of it, yet which sits within it with absolute rightness.

The plaza forms neither narrow alleys nor squares or grand vistas but a flowing space that swells and compresses. It is easy to navigate but also meandering. We too like spaces that have this sense of informality and transition.

The Smithsons were cerebral architects but also cared immensely about the quality of the built detail. Everything is considered without being over-complicated. The baroque gorgeousness of the stone is revealed by it being left unpolished and unsealed, and the joints are expressed with deep grooves — but of course this is countered by the clean lines and the detailing.

There are relatively few projects where the physical experience genuinely conveys the theoretical bent of the architect, but here the

way the Smithsons thought about the character of the spaces between buildings and the neutral, almost generic nature of the buildings themselves is clearly felt on the ground. It was a test case for ideas that they were developing more widely in their Berlin work and elsewhere, working towards an idiom that was expressive of the time, creating a different form of city space 'for a cognitive society that would be in control of its direction'.

While on one level it is very English in being perhaps polite, reserved and unshowy, on the other hand, the space is perhaps more American, a little version of the big plazas of New York City developments that take up a whole block. I like this ambition to be more than just another version of what has always existed in the city.

Despite their listed status and place in the architectural canon, the Economist buildings still get under the establishment's skin – a 2008 report commissioned by the St James's Conservation Trust recommended delisting and redevelopment in a more appropriate' form.

Half a century on, the Economist project still has the power to unsettle.

The Bank building with the Economist tower to the rear. Together with a smaller residential tower, these three buildings form the Economist Plaza.

View past the Economist tower through the plaza to the Bank building. The plaza has a flowing and meandering quality that Tom Grieve and Hana Loftus admire.

27

QUIET SUBVERSION The Economist Plaza was Alison and Peter Smithson's most universally acclaimed work, completed relatively early in their chequered career between Hunstanton School and Robin Hood Gardens.

Commissioned to design new offices for the Economist in the heart of establishment St James's, the architects devised a cluster of three concrete-framed buildings connected by a raised podium with an irregular-shaped public plaza. The middle-sized Bank Building is positioned on the most prominent corner site in front of the largest component, the 16-storey Economist block. A residential tower for Boodle's is at the back of the site. Each block is faced in roach Portland stone with a high fossil content and is chamfered to soften its relationship to the others.

The complex was Grade II* listed in 1988.

Two of the three Economist plaza buildings. The taller tower houses offices while the shorter one is residential.

Edgar Gonzalez of Brisac Gonzalez in the main conference room of the Communist Party headquarters in Paris.

Communist Party Headquarters

Location: Paris, France
Architect: Oscar Niemeyer
Completed: 1967–80
Chosen by Edgar Gonzalez of Brisac Gonzalez

I'm Cuban-born and like most Cubans who manage to leave, the last thing you want to visit is something Communist! But with Oscar Niemeyer's French Communist Party building, I was interested in it from an architectural, not a political, perspective.

I first visited the building in 1985, when I was studying in Vicenza at the Centro Internazionale di Studi di Architettura Andrea Palladio, and I have been back three times since. Because I was overdosing on Palladian architecture, I thought I'd go to Paris and escape from northern Italian Renaissance architecture to something rather more contemporary. I'd seen the French Communist Party headquarters in books on Niemeyer and around that time had visited the Interbau apartments in Berlin – his take on Le Corbusier's' Unité d'Habitation. It's an anomaly to find this kind of architecture in the historic centres of European cities, especially in Paris.

What I like most is that it's old school. It's not trying to be witty or clever. It doesn't pay homage to other buildings. The building incorporates interesting structural solutions, but they are not the main attraction. It's an exercise in space – it's sculptural, but beyond a simplistic object.

For me, the best part is how this S-shaped building appears to be holding back the very dense Parisian street fabric in order to create an open space at the corner of the site overlooking Place du Colonel Fabien. Inside, the point where the dome meets the sloping floor is great; there is a nice dynamic between the two geometries. The office block feels very light as it appears to hover above the ground, The way a building meets the ground is very important in our work too.

Many buildings have grand stairs that one walks up, but here you walk down a fairly humble staircase. The stairs lead into a somewhat James Bond-like underground space, which is the main foyer. Conventionally, it's not what you would call a spectacular space or a beautiful space – there is little natural light and no views out, but once you get over that, it is very pleasant and architecturally very rich. It's an exercise in the manipulation of space without natural light through elements such as the unusual undulating floor, the reflective mirrored walls, and highly tactile in-situ concrete walls. The furniture is also fantastic. The floor is pretty wild – you wouldn't get away with it now – and gives a really interesting spatial effect. If you had a flat floor instead, the underground space would be very oppressive and you'd go a bit crazy in there.

Being by Niemeyer, there's lots of in-situ concrete including these planar columns that are very sculptural, and you can see the nice shuttering detail. This texture softens up the concrete which would otherwise look a bit bland. I really like the built-in furniture which has in-situ concrete lined with leather cushions.

The main conference hall ceiling is reminiscent of Paco Rabanne's spherical disc dresses from the sixties. You would've have seen lots of suspended ceiling tiles like that in seventies airports. Here the ceiling is made of hundreds of strips of chemically treated metal to improve the acoustics and the light quality.

I hadn't noticed until I went back on our revisit how these panels animate the space just enough for you to forget you are in an enclosed dome with no access to the outside. And even though it's artificial light, the quality is actually quite good.

I've always liked that the building has several different temperaments. After the cavernous underground areas which feel very secure, you move up into the offices which feel very light and inviting, with two long sides of glass curtain walling bookended by solid ends of ceramic tiles. The single-glazed façade can be opened. Then there's the roof terrace which is a fairly sculptural element quite different from other parts of the building, with areas cut out to allow light into what was the top-floor café.

The main way it has influenced me is in terms of how a building can use architecture to create new urban space on a site. For the National Academy of Arts competition we did in Bergen, the idea of creating new civic space around the building is one that, subconciously or not, was influenced by Niemeyer's work.

In our proposal for a cultural centre in Sainte-Maxime in the south of France, the building's periphery created an oasis of open space in a former quarry. I've never really linked our Aberdeen visual arts centre project to Niemeyer's building, but the terracing does create more public space above the submerged accommodation than the current hillside. The Communist Party Headquarters had a more direct specific influence at the Museum of World Culture in Gothenburg, Sweden, where we used similarly expressive shuttering on the stairs and a large mushroom-like column.

The Paris headquarters is a sculptural building with many intricacies which also creates an open space in the city centre. It's more than a one-liner. For me, along with Jean Nouvel's Fondation Cartier, it is one of two buildings in Paris that I'll return to again and again. They are very different, but both use architecture to create unique urban conditions.

PARTY PIECE Oscar Niemeyer's stunning headquarters for the French Communist Party in Paris was commissioned in the late 1960s – a time when the Communists enjoyed great popularity in France.

A Communist himself, Niemeyer waived his fee for the building. Visitors enter the building down a small flight of steps into the main foyer space. This strange, undulating landscape, intended to suggest a hillside, leads to the main conference hall whose white domed roof rises up out of the forecourt. Above ground, Niemeyer built six floors of offices in a gently waving plan, with a curtain-walled façade designed in conjunction with engineer Jean Prouvé. Views down from the roof terrace suggest the shape of a hammer and sickle in the landscape of the forecourt.

Niemeyer's building and original furnishings have survived largely intact. The Communist Party no longer occupies all the office floors, and has converted the top floor café for office use.

Opposite: The white dome of the basement conference hall contrasts with the slick curtain walling of the main office building behind.

Above: A concrete-walled corridor in one of the building's underground floors, which contain car parking and meeting rooms.

Left: The main conference hall ceiling is dominated by hundreds of hanging metal ceiling tiles that improve acoustics and light quality.

Above: One of the underground meeting rooms, with exposed concrete walls and acoustic hanging ceiling tiles.

Right: Visitors descend into a gently undulating entrance foyer designed to evoke a hillside. Much of Niemeyer's original furniture survives.

Jonathan Ellis-Miller
in front of the hi-tech
Schlumberger Cambridge
Research Centre.

Schlumberger Cambridge Research Centre

Location: Cambridge, UK
Architect: Hopkins Architects
Built: 1985–92

Chosen by Jonathan Ellis-Miller of EllisMiller Architects

I was born in the Cambridgeshire Fens and was driving home from university on the A14 when I first saw it. It was extraordinarily peculiar, like a giant spider that had just landed.

It's such a novelty in the flat Fenland landscape, a beacon in the tradition of great East Anglian churches such as Ely Cathedral. This is fantastic motorway architecture – a building that has impact when you view it at 70mph and has the notion of something odd, extraordinary and truly modern. But it exists on so many different levels of interest apart from that dramatic, fleeting motorway view, from the way it sits in the landscape right down to the detail of the furniture in the winter garden.

When it was built, it was a hugely optimistic building that said something about the future, and I think it still does. This building celebrates research and industry – and, as a theatre of exciting technology, it is entirely right that its form is theatrical rather than a faceless building with no personality. I've always thought it would make a great building for a baddie in a Roger Moore-era James Bond film.

When I first saw the Schlumberger building, I was studying architecture at Liverpool and at the time there was a real interest in hi-tech coming from tutors Alan Brookes and Dave King. Hopkins' work naturally resonated with me – not just Schlumberger but the earlier house in Hampstead.

I've never been as expressively hi-tech as Hopkins was at Schlumberger, but for me its appeal isn't about style, but about how that building is made and organised, and how the programme follows the slightly strange function of what goes on there. The hi-tech wrapping is entirely appropriate for the building's activities as a highly specific environment for top-notch scientists.

It's a proper modern building dictated by 'form follows function' yet it is highly crafted and deeply classical in terms of its symmetry. The whole building concept came out of what went on inside.

Every element is considered. It is utterly non-whimsical yet the result is beautifully poetic, in particular the relationship to the landscape. Part of its drama is the discovery of the building as you approach and its contrast with the countryside. The building, once glimpsed, only reveals itself once you have turned off the main road. It sits in an almost bucolic meadow, replete with sheep. This setting only enhances the building's otherworldliness.

Plan aesthetic is important to me and this plan is beautiful, very legible and entirely practical. It's fascinating how Hopkins resolves the dirty and dangerous cheek by jowl with the theory and practice.

The building is organised in three elements. The central tensile fabric spine contains the social areas and the main research facilities. On each side of the central spine are two pavilions that have cellular offices, with views over the landscape with laboratories and breakout spaces on the inside face.

The public entrance to the building is at the southern end and the service entrance is at the northern end. The building is then subdivided into five individual pavilions, each division expressed through the structure of the building. The divisions mark cross routes in a deliberate move to encourage lateral movement across the building. This is a building where its users are actively encouraged by the architecture to have the opportunity for casual meetings.

This was the last of the lightweight Hopkins buildings. Like the Hopkins House in Hampstead, it's a mix of cheap industrial materials put together really precisely. They've used no more material than needs to be used. The cladding, for example, is a cheap corrugated material with a profile that avoids having to have, or pay for, a drip. For what it provides, this is a very economical building.

The design is utterly disciplined, full of detail and completely dimensionally co-ordinated, right down to the way the floor tiles line up with the structure in the winter garden. To really appreciate it, you have to enjoy structure and the way you see the structure coming in through the envelope and how the detail is brought through.

It's standing the test of time well. I think there's still a real freshness about Schlumberger – a sense of timeless modernity. It's amazing how much of the original interior is retained considering there's such a moveable feast of research going on there. I also think that innovations in solar technology will make lightweight constructions like this much more possible.

Along with the Sainsbury Centre (see pp94–97), PA Technology Center, the Pompidou Centre and the Lloyd's Building, Schlumberger is one of the few true icons of hi-tech architecture. But, for me, Schlumberger was followed by an addition by the same architect that was not so good. Rather than following through the ideas of the first building, in the later entrance building (1992), Hopkins got into different territory and lost the poetry of the first.

Coming back to visit, I find it hilarious how blindingly obvious – though subliminal – the influence on EllisMiller's work has been in terms of its plan aesthetic and organisation of space. My mentor John Winter once taught Michael Hopkins at the Architectural Association so perhaps it's inevitable that we share a sense of the deeply practical, which this kind of building is all about. It's particularly clear in our design for Catmose College in Oakham. Like Schlumberger, we have a central spine that contains the social and practical functions of the school with pavilions on either side containing classroom clusters with large breakout spaces. The main central atrium space has a bridge, just as the Schlumberger test hall has a bridge at the far end.

Schlumberger is an absolute corker of a building – fun to look at but a class act for sure and probably, along with Lloyd's, one of the most important of recent modern buildings.

Entrance atrium, with glimpses through to the test hall beyond, which is flanked by laboratories.

HI-TECH PIONEER Hopkins Architects won a competition to design an experimental test facility for Schlumberger's oil-drilling divisions in 1983. The site, a rubbish dump in Victorian times, was on the western outskirts of Cambridge. Schlumberger wanted a building that spoke of technology and made a hi-tech statement. As well as providing natural light, the lightweight roof that soared over the test hall had another important practical function – in the unlikely case of an explosion, it would rip first before the windows blew out and so would cause less damage than broken glass.

The building was completed in 1985. Visitors enter into a winter garden that doubles as the staff canteen. Beyond is the test hall, with laboratories on either side and offices on the perimeter with full-height sliding glazed doors to maximise views of the Fens. There are red accents throughout the interior on door handles, ventilation covers and laboratory shelving.

A second smaller building, also designed by Hopkins Architects, was completed in 1992. Between them, the two buildings house 140 staff.

Above right: The lightweight steel structure is fully expressed with a series of masts supporting the tensile roof.

Above left: Detail of mast structure. The building's hi-tech expression celebrates the research and technology of its function.

Graham Haworth of
Haworth Tompkins outside
the "uplifting" Erco
Technical Centre.

Erco Technical Centre

Location: Lüdenscheid, Germany

Architect: Uwe Kiessler

Completed: 1985–88

Chosen by Graham Haworth of Haworth Tompkins

I first saw the Erco building in the late 1980s on a road trip through Germany, not long after it had been finished. It has been at the back of my mind ever since, coming to the foreground again recently when Haworth Tompkins designed the Dyson Building for the Royal College of Art in Battersea, south London.

Erco Technical Centre was a touchstone for the Dyson Building. We saw that building as a place of production – an art factory. James Dyson's involvement and his campaign for more investment in innovation made me reflect on the value of buildings that provide thoughtful support for the creative work of others. Erco's Technical Centre is proof positive of the success of this approach.

Much contemporary architectural energy focuses on form-making. I wanted to present a building that successfully prioritises issues that tend to get overlooked, such as function, technology, ecology and sustainability. To be utilitarian and functional sounds dull and boring, but that is not the case with this building. It has an authenticity about it. It restores your faith in modernism. Yet people are often scared of doing things that are this simple in approach.

The client and owner of the Erco lighting company, Klaus Jürgen Maack, wanted a building that could provide what he called 'overalls for engineers' – tough, flexible and loose-fitting, but comfortable and rather elegant too – that would encourage communication between people and enable them to get on with their work in the best way.

Maack was interested in extending Erco's 1960s HQ in a contemporary way. His brief for the Technical Centre called for an egalitarian

building that did not express a hierarchical ranking and instead broke down boundaries between management and workforce.

For Kiessler, working with an enlightened client who used the best graphic designers (notably Otl Aicher) and industrial designers must have been the perfect job. It was to be a close client-architect dialogue – when they needed to decide the size of the handrails, they took a walk through the woods and picked up pieces of wood to try.

The result is an eloquent expression of how the Technical Centre is put together. Each component looks as if it has been placed there by hand and bolted in place with an arts & crafts understanding of how a building is made, which we too always try to get into our buildings. There is absolute clarity.

While the British approach to hi-tech moved towards the slickly finished and over-manicured, in this building Kiessler offers something different – raw and unfinished in comparison and uncompromisingly technical in its execution, but with a human scale.

Kiessler achieved this through the manipulation of section and exploitation of visual connections to create a generosity of space, with split levels and double-height spaces. He avoided making adaptable workplaces into anonymous generic volumes and instead provided a specific and complex spatial and sectional arrangement.

There is also a clear external expression of how the building works: horizontal louvres over sloped glazing, external brise-soleil blinds on the south-facing façades, large travelling jibs, gantries and sliding access ladders to reach

every element of the envelope that requires regular cleaning. This is probably why the building is in such good shape – the horizontal corrugated aluminium is incredibly beautiful and still looks fresh.

The flow of spaces is immediately apparent on entering the central hall beneath the tower. This enables views into other spaces where different activities are taking place. While specific, these have a provisional nature to them that is open to change.

Kiessler also celebrates imperfection. A bridge several floors up joins his building to the 1960s block and, because the floors don't line up, the bridge slopes and enters both buildings off the anticipated right angle. Elsewhere, elements and geometries collide, fold or taper.

What is not immediately apparent is how the building effortlessly fits into the steeply sloping site. The central tower splits it into two distinct, offset wings and this geometry allows a specific relationship with its site context. A large car park is hidden by the clever manipulation of the site gradient and access road.

I would describe Kiessler's approach as 'ecological' in the sense of 'a branch of science concerned with the inter-relationship of organisms and their environments'. And so the technik is tempered not only in its response to human scale, but also in its juxtaposition to nature.

The building never actually touches the landscape – this is always done through a series of retaining elements or stepped terraces in stone or concrete, now wonderfully overgrown with ivy and Virginia creeper. The glazed ends of the main tooling shop and design studio allow

the landscape of the surrounding countryside to visually enter, and between his building and the 1960s block Kiessler created a series of densely planted courtyard spaces.

The visible flat roofs on the east and west wings, between the glazed halls, are planted green roofs, which were pioneering at the time.

The park-like company grounds are designed to be close to nature.

Every time you walk into the Erco Technical Centre, it feels uplifting – with an openness and a great quality of light, even on an overcast day like today. It feels like a clean slate. I just wish I'd designed this building.

Main entrance. Graham Haworth admires the building's simple yet elegant utilitarianism and functionality.

TECHNICAL PRECISION The brief for architect Uwe Kiessler (born 1937) when designing the Erco Technical Centre was to create a building that would be an expression of the company culture. Completed in 1988 at the lighting company's headquarters at Lüdenscheid, the highly transparent and functional building embodied a carefully controlled corporate identity that extends to the type and colour of flowers used in all its global offices.

Its purpose was to provide a greater production area by moving non-productive departments of the company together in a special building, and adding the freed areas to the production area. These departments included tool-making, photometric and electrical laboratories, plus design and marketing. As such, the building is an extension to the large, 100m-wide 1960s production department behind and links to it through the existing administrative building at three levels. Erco has since further extended the complex and the site now houses 800 staff.

Above left: Generous office windows give views over the technical complex and the surrounding landscape.

Above right: Detail of spiral escape staircase at the rear of the main tooling shop.

Education

Clare Wright in the library at Charles Rennie
Mackintosh's masterpiece, the Glasgow School of Art.

Glasgow School Of Art

Location: Glasgow, UK
Architect: Charles Rennie Mackintosh
Built: 1896–1909
Chosen by Clare Wright of Wright & Wright Architects

I've encountered the Glasgow School of Art at different times in my life – as a school child, as an architecture student there and later as an external examiner. Each time I have been deeply affected by it – you think differently about it when you've had more life experience. It's an incredibly complex building that can be read at many levels.

My first experience of the Mac was as a child of about 12 when I went there for art classes. This was something of a coming-of-age experience. At a time when my family was going through some painful events I went off and signed up for classes by myself, which was quite a big deal. I come from a very academic family and art hadn't been on the agenda. It may be a collective experience but my memory is that when I went inside the building I was deeply moved and invigorated. I think great pieces of art often touch the unconscious in a primal way – a sort of dream world. The building certainly lit me up and gave me a feeling of euphoria. I felt it validated my own creativity and that I could be myself. It was a personal world to me away from school, which I found very boring, and one to which I felt I really belonged.

We used to play in the building as well as paint – it was Saturday morning and we were the only ones there. We had a game where we had to get down the whole of the east staircase without touching the stairs by wriggling through the holes in the central wall. We were working in the eyrie of the hen run and we used to jump along it to make the cantilever bounce, gobsmacked by the panoramic views of Glasgow. My feelings about the building were intensely emotive and a reminder to me now years later that untrained people, including children, can appreciate and be influenced by architecture.

It is an extraordinary building in many ways. It is complex but the construction detailing is simple. It is robust literally and figuratively. Contemporary spaces for others' creativity are often neutral – white galleries and black auditoria. The Mac evokes creativity by being a powerful presence to kick against that is not too precious or controlling. It cannot easily be damaged even by 100 years of teenagers' artistic mess.

I went to study architecture at the Mac when I was 16 and met my partner, Sandy Wright, there. We were very lucky to be taught by Andy MacMillan and Isi Metzstein and very privileged to learn close up and day to day, from their take on the building.

Going back as a mature architect I appreciate the rationality of the plan combined with the richness of the section, although the plan isn't simple. The entrance is bang in the middle of the front elevation, with north-facing studios either side but with asymmetrically arranged windows. Principal spaces are in the middle and at the east and west ends but each is different.

There are countless spatial sequences, with thematic echoes in the building. Mackintosh plays a lot with transition and boundaries and that's something that has preoccupied us in our work at Wright & Wright too.

As with the best of Corb and Aalto I am most moved by the humanity of the building – its tactility and amazing details. Everything's black and white except for tiny touches of colour such as the stained glass in the doors and the tiles on the stairs. Each is unique – the tiles are slightly smudged or not quite straight. There is a nuanced repetition of form and colour – it's immensely playful.

Light is manipulated with absolute mastery. I like the darkness of many of the spaces – when you come into the white rooms in the Mackintosh they are rich through contrast. All the studios have excellent, appropriate north or top light, even in the basement.

Mackintosh showed the same skill in his handling of materials, playing with them until they become abstractions that resonate.

The library is my favourite space. When I was a student, there was a spell when I went there in the summer evenings to enjoy the peace. It is one of the greatest spaces in the world – I was very lucky to be able to chain smoke up there, basking in the west light, while thumbing through bound architectural magazines looking for inspiration! Now, it's largely shut to students.

The library is like a building inside a building. There is the most amazing layering of space so it's impossible to say where the edges are. Stepping into one of the window bays is like the opposite of stepping off a cliff, with the space spiralling, unexpectedly, above you through an extra storey.

Mackintosh's timber detailing is exquisite. He makes you forget that he is just joining wood together and you see the shapes, the movement and the curves, the solids and the voids. When he starts to nibble away at the uprights and with each carved facet in a different colour, he's really playing.

The west elevation that fronts the library is a masterpiece with the power of Beethoven. It's extraordinary, with the staccato of the small windows at the top, and the deep notes of the three long windows for the library, edged with great rolls of masonry and rippling off on

smaller formation to the side only to fold back into the plane of the façade. All are terminated with a merging of the inside and the outside as the building stretches out to create a level platform at the door, as if to catch students going down the 1:4 hill.

It's quite difficult to talk about being influenced by Mackintosh because all of us who studied there were. There are, of course, links to our work. Wright & Wright's buildings tend to be very rational in plan with lots happening in section. They are about light and using materials in a way that's true to their nature. We like contrasts between compression and expansion and between light and dark, and we design spaces that have ambiguous boundaries.

I like to use tones of darkness. We did this in the Women's Library and at Hull Truck Theatre, where we decided consciously to have a dark building and made the whole thing a black box from the outside in using rough and ready materials – black on black.

The Mac always reinvigorates me as I know it does others. Perhaps the greatest achievement for an architect is to build something that makes other people come alive.

The library – Clare Wright's favourite space at the Glasgow School of Art – with its distinctive pendant lights and timber detailing.

MACKINTOSH MASTERPIECE The Glasgow School of Art was Charles Rennie Mackintosh's first and most important commission. He won the project in competition in 1896 while working at the Glasgow architectural practice of Honeyman and Keppie and completed the Art Nouveau masterpiece in 1909. The rich and eclectic interiors, including the iconic library with its triple-height windows, were created in collaboration with his wife, the designer Margaret Macdonald. Clare Wright revisited the building before it was severely damaged by fire in 2014. It is currrently undergoing restoration. It is Category A listed.

Main entrance. The eclectic design of the building includes the influence of Scottish baronial architecture as well as Art Nouveau.

Basement studio. All the studios in the building are excellently lit with either north or top lighting.

View up of the triple-height window bay in the library. To the left are examples of the notched timber detailing throughout the space.

Cranbrook's campus is arranged around a lake overlooked by a grand portico. Edward Jones admires the faithful realisation of the generous masterplan.

Cranbrook Academy Of Art

Location: near Detroit, Michigan, USA
Architect: Eliel Saarinen
Completed: 1928–42
Chosen by Edward Jones of Dixon Jones

Saarinen (father Eliel and son Eero) and Cranbrook have held a lasting place in my architectural memory. The first encounter was in 1957 at Eero Saarinen's General Motors Tech Center in Detroit, the Versailles of the automotive styling industry.

Later in 1961, I worked a long summer for Eero, under the watchful eye of Cesar Pelli on Lincoln Center's Repertory Theater. It was then that I discovered Cranbrook down the road and attended life-drawing classes there in the evenings. This inspiring institution was in contrast to the world of drag racing and honky tonk in nearby Woodward Avenue with its bars from where the Motown sound originated (also highly enjoyable).

The other contrast was the nature of Eliel Saarinen's architecture at Cranbrook. Unlike his son's practice where 'a style for the job' was the philosophy, here Eliel's architecture was a restrained modern classicism. It was completed in 1942, and interestingly when less benign regimes elsewhere were favouring a not dissimilar architectural enthusiasm. Despite being privately funded there was also an atmosphere of Franklin D Roosevelt's New Deal about the place.

Cranbrook's founder, the Detroit newspaper publisher George Booth, commissioned Eliel Saarinen to design the Academy of Art buildings in 1928 and in 1932 made him President of the Academy, giving him control to realise his plan. The focus of the campus is the open Portico, flanked by the library and museum on either side and facing a long rectangular lake which establishes a large-scale ordering device for the campus as a whole. Either side of the lake are studios and student/

staff houses including Saarinen's own, elegantly planned house and garden. The arrangement is not unlike the University of Virginia, where the lake acts as a substitute for Thomas Jefferson's great lawn.

Cranbrook is a glorious place but what is it that is so inspiring? It might be said that there was a lot of scraped classicism around at the time; the Carl Milles sculptures dancing in their fountains are charming, verging on the cute; and the total design of the late Jugendstil arts and crafts was never my enthusiasm. What makes Cranbrook inspiring is the realisation of a generous idea. Too often, well-intentioned masterplans are subverted by others who do not share the original conception. But at Cranbrook Eliel Saarinen was architect of the first move and he could therefore control the outcome with its clear urban hierarchies and material distinctions between houses and studios for students (brick), and library and museums for the academy (stone). In addition the landscape with its marvellous stepped lake has triumphed, looking towards the south into a distant and enigmatic perspective.

Rafael Moneo has suggested that it might be an exaggeration to say that Cranbrook is the American equivalent of the Bauhaus. However in this civilised place Charles Eames and Eero Saarinen collaborated on those early plywood shelled chairs, and Florence Knoll, Harry Bertoia and Fumihiko Maki were among the many other notable alumni. It is one of the curiosities of America that such places of cultivation can flourish without the energy of an accompanying metropolitan centre.

I returned 20 years later in the mid 1980s when I was building the Mississauga Civic Centre on

the outskirts of Toronto and when the scale and generosity of Cranbrook provided further reassurance to this Canadian adventure. I was fully prepared for the decline and devastation of Detroit but was pleasantly surprised to find Cranbrook in the best of health. More recently I visited in 2010 to review extension works by a new generation of architects thoughtfully commissioned by Cranbrook. With each addition, the purpose of Saarinen's original plan for George Booth has been enriched. The comparison with the Bauhaus might be no exaggeration after all.

CREATIVE CAMPUS Part of the Cranbrook Educational Community, Cranbrook Academy of Art was founded by Detroit newspaper baron and philanthropist George Gough Booth. He hired Finnish architect Eliel Saarinen to oversee the architectural and landscape development of the campus (1925–1941) and installed him as president of the Academy of Art in 1932.

Designed as an inspirational setting for creativity, the campus is a complex of small buildings arranged in a tight plan in a landscaped park. Built in brick and stone, the buildings are notable for their fine Arts and Crafts detailing. An exception is the sparser, abstracted classicism of the Academy art museum and library, Saarinen's last major work at Cranbrook.

More recently, additional buildings have been added to the campus by Rafael Moneo, Steven Holl, Tod Williams and Billie Tsien, and Peter Rose.

Jon Buck (left) and Dominic Cullinan (right) at the University of Leicester Engineering Building.

University of Leicester Engineering Building

Location: Leicester, UK
Architect: Stirling & Gowan
Completed: 1959–63
Chosen by Jon Buck and Dominic Cullinan of SCABAL Architects

Jon Buck

I did my degree at South Bank University and as a busy undergraduate you'd see a picture of a building fleetingly in a lecture and decide on just that if you liked it or not. Before I saw the slide of the Leicester Engineering Building showing the main auditorium projecting out, it had never even occurred to me that something on the inside could have so much impact on the outside.

By the time I was 19, James Stirling was my favourite architect, mainly because of that auditorium. Stirling's work was always difficult and I was drawn to this, in the same way that I was drawn to John McEnroe rather than Björn Borg. At architecture school in the eighties, you either went down the post-modernist route or you liked Richard Meier, Richard Rogers and hi-tech instead. But Stirling was both a modernist and a post-modernist and I couldn't let go of him. Sometimes I loathed his work but at the same time I was drawn to it. I also wanted to be able to create something that was that difficult and discordant.

While my early relationship with the building had been through the auditorium, when I later saw photos of the Toblerone roof lights on the workshop I realised there were so many more aspects to it, and so many inconsistencies – the best things about it. The building does feel incredibly English.

Unlike Stirling's Staatsgallerie Stuttgart, Leicester Engineering Building wasn't a letdown when I visited. Instead it was flawed, but magnificent. I'm delighted with the discovery that the architects weren't precious about the details, and I'm delighted with the penicillin pink handrails which work so well against the concrete steps, though maybe not so well against the terracotta. There are also the chamfers – in order to get softness and interest in a plan we still go there first, knocking corners off until we get the right chamfer. It feels like a very friendly experience.

We're meant to be impressed by it from the outside, but I'm impressed by it inside. I find it very delicate – the architects have filled the space beneath the water tower at the top with a great deal of tenderness. There are just a few simple ideas, then the detail gets on with itself.

The thing that strikes me most is its tininess and spatial generosity. I want to live on the landings – there is something very domestic about them. The quality of light is of a kind you only get between very solid masses.

The engineering block is something you can cuddle rather than something that overawes you. When I was 18, I thought it was heroic and barnstorming and about five times bigger than it actually is. Instead, it's small and delicate, and that's what appeals to me now. It was before hi-tech, which was obsessed with engineering and the authenticity that structure gives to your building. This is interested in other things but just happens to be an engineering building. Hi-tech has gone out of fashion, but this building hasn't.

Dominic Cullinan

This is not a building I've always had a deep knowledge of – it feels more like the words to a Madonna song that you just know without ever learning them because you can hear it everywhere.

Visiting it for the first time, in a strange way it seems totally familiar. The language of the building is so commonly used now, and I'm reminded how many times you see its likeness. Its clear expression of content and its shapeliness, its fluidity, its elegant lines, as well as its generally apparent easy design.

It's so inside-turned-out, a very visceral building, almost intestinal with its blood colours and oesophagus staircases complete with fluid pipes running up inside them – like an anatomical diagram occupied. It's a body.

It's very idiosyncratic in that its design takes on a lot of the imagery of engineering but in a naive way. They're discovering a connection for the first time between architecture and engineering before hi-tech made a fetish of it. But this is done in a very sophisticated manner and, without being cynical; it does manage to openly display its authorship and a deep sense of knowing. Maybe this is why the current head of engineering, Professor John Fothergill, calls it Stirling's first post-modern building.

Its smallness and interconnectivity is what makes it special for me. I'm impressed that this great icon of engineering and architecture is actually a very tiny, dinky thing although at the time I bet they thought it was huge and majestic. Because it's so small, you almost think you're in a single dwelling when you're inside the engineer's house. It's great that it's preserved as nicely as it is.

But one of its problems is that it's a very finished piece of work. Nowadays, and you can see this on the campus around it, buildings are (and should be) expected to be able to grow and distort – people say 'morph' – in response to their changing fortunes, like engineering

itself. But this one is so precise and perfectly conceived as a limited object. But it's so wonderful it could be as wonderful even it had to be empty.

Visiting Leicester Engineering Building is a nice day out that reminds us of who we want to be. Looking at the building back then as students we were looking at the possible ideal of what it was to be an architect. One day it will surely be our turn.

We will be asked by intelligent people operating at the meeting point between the academic and the practical to design them a building not only ideally representing but actually accommodating that precise place – intelligence, good looks and physical activity – making things work.

That idea or ideal remains strong in our minds and still clearly defines what we would like ourselves to be as gentlemen architects.

Above: Bright pink handrails and informal seating on the landing overlooking the main entrance. Jon Buck and Dominic Cullinan admire the building's "domestic" quality.

Opposite: The Engineering Faculty combines laboratories and workshops (right) with a tower (left) containing offices above lecture theatres on the lower three floors.

STIRLING WORK Leicester Engineering Faculty was Stirling & Gowan's last building as a partnership. It had an immediate and enduring impact, proving hugely influential in both its structural feats and its knowing referencing of modern movement forms from a generation earlier. For this reason, it has often been considered the first post-modernist building in the UK.

The building consists of a tower plus adjacent laboratories and workshops covered in a saw-tooth glass roof. The tower's lower three floors are taken up by two projecting lecture theatres. On the southern side are laboratories from floors three to six. In the main 11-storey tower each floor contains four offices for teaching staff, with the exception of the head of department's office, which takes up floor six and the water tank on the top floor. It now serves 600 students, twice the number it was designed for.

The building was Grade II* listed in 1993. It has had considerable maintenance issues over the decades, in particular its leaking windows and roofs, plus difficulties with heating and cooling, and glazing.

Niall McLaughlin at Trinity College's Berkeley Library, the building that made him want to be an architect.

Berkeley Library, Trinity College

Location: Dublin, Ireland

Architect: Ahrends Burton Koralek

Completed: 1960–67

Chosen by Niall McLaughlin of Niall McLaughlin Architects

Berkeley Library was very influential on me becoming an architect. It was the first time I felt architecture could speak to me.

It was the summer before I went to study at university. I'd opted to study English at Trinity. I was 17. I didn't study art. I didn't draw. I didn't have any understanding of architecture. But I was spending time around the campus and was very interested in the library, and at the same time the Goulding Summerhouse in Enniskerry by Scott Tallon Walker, which was near my home. They both seemed to be incredibly glamorous. They had an extraordinary high focus that I couldn't articulate at the time.

I remember walking through the campus and stopping to look at these amazing curved windows. I climbed up to them to get a closer look and this guy stopped and started talking to me about them, and got me thinking about architecture. It wasn't until a year later when I came to study at University College Dublin, I realised he was actually the architectural historian Brendan Murphy.

After this encounter, I remember saying to a friend of mine that I might be interested in architecture. At the end of the summer you have a sort of last chance saloon to apply for a different course and with last-minute intuition, I chose architecture. I got an interview purely on my exam results and when I was asked about the buildings I liked, the library was the one I talked about.

Certain buildings have an extraordinary vividness, a sense of being more intense than others. That special presence is renewed every time I see the building. It seems to communicate to me in a quite different way to language.

I think what's great is the sculptural power of the building as an artefact. The neighbouring Deane & Woodward-designed Trinity College Museum is a brilliant Ruskinian building and the library needed to hold its own against that. ABK's library is entirely of its time but contextually situated. When it was completed, it was criticised for not being extendable, for being a finite object. But I think that was right – they could, and did, build another finite object next to it. When you see the building now, 40 or 50 years later, it has become a historic artefact in the city as well.

It is incredible that it was done by three people who were just starting to feel their way as a practice. The relationship between the plastic qualities of the in-situ concrete, the taut skin of the granite and the liquid qualities of the glass is impressive. For me, this curved glass is incredibly lush and for a 1960s building, such a Victorian thing.

It's only since I came to London that I understand better the terms of reference from which the library came. I was reading an essay on La Tourette by Corbusier and I realised there was a huge tranche of projects cascading down from it, including the Berkeley Library and Lasdun's Royal College of Physicians.

Like La Tourette, the library isn't sitting on the landscape but appears to be above it, dropping down so that it's barely resting on it. The building establishes itself at the top with the planar granite walls and then recedes back in steps towards the ground rather than vice versa. That's what lets it punch its weight.

I recently met up with the ABK partners and what was very touching was Richard Burton recalling when he got a telegram from Paul Koralek in New York saying he had won the library competition and wanted to come back to do the building with Burton and Peter Ahrends. He felt this tremendous gratitude from him that the promise they'd made to themselves as AA students of setting up in practice had been kept. For me, who'd have liked to have gone into practice with someone myself but didn't find anyone to do so, seeing the three AKB founders' pleasure in each other's company, their generosity, and their lack of ego was great.

When I think of it, I always go back to its confident sense of massing and also the fine details like the suppression of the window sills. I think about the very exact relationship between the stone, bronze shutters and projections of glass. But I haven't applied it literally to a project.

Perhaps the project I have designed that takes most from this experience is the competition-winning scheme for Castleford Museum & Library. The idea of taking a book from the illuminated centre and moving to a particular seat at the edge, the stepping back in of arrayed window seats and the beehive-like texture of the space are, perhaps, memories of that original experience. Sadly, my library was not built.

But the Berkeley Library was the building that made me want to be an architect.

Whenever I come back to Dublin, I always pass through Trinity. For me, the library has weathered and just got better and better. The juxtaposition of its very simple surfaces with the deeply sculptured façade of its neighbour is to me still a very, very powerful architectural moment.

LIBRARY LEARNING Trinity College Library was the building that kick-started the acclaimed architectural practice Ahrends Burton Koralek (ABK). The new library was the first to be built at Trinity College since the 1930s. It accommodates reading places for 470 and book storage for up to 830,000 volumes.

The site was between the old eighteenth-century library and the nineteenth-century museum. ABK's new building was positioned on a podium to create a forecourt between the two older buildings. On the ground floor is the catalogue and reference section while the first and second floors create one double-height reading room plus a choice of large and small study spaces with different degrees of enclosure and light. In the forecourt fronting the north elevation, a series of light shafts provides illumination for the basement accommodation.

ABK subsequently built again at the university, completing the Arts Building in 1979 and an extension to this in 2003.

Clad in granite, the Berkeley Library was built between the college's eighteenth-century library and nineteenth-century museum.

Above left: Architects ABK designed a range of large and small study spaces with varying degrees of enclosure and light to give choice to users.

Above right: View up from the double-height reading room. As well as top-lit spaces, the library offers generous views of the surrounding gardens through the large curved glass bay windows on the west façade.

St Catherine's College, Oxford

Location: Oxford, UK
Architect: Arne Jacobsen
Completed: 1962–68
Chosen by Rab and Denise Bennetts of Bennetts Associates

Denise (left) and Rab (right) Bennetts in the main quad at St Catherine's College, Oxford, which they first visited as students.

Rab Bennetts

We first came here in 1975 when we were studying at the Edinburgh College of Art. We had a year out working in London and decided to spend our last weekend before heading back to Edinburgh sprinting around Oxford and Cambridge looking at new buildings such as St Catherine's College and ABK's Keble College. St Catherine's turned out to have a lasting influence on our career. It's all done with restraint, the minimum number of elements and materials, with everything beautifully executed. It's extraordinarily refined. Jacobsen showed you don't need to show off to get recognition.

None of the buildings are shouting for attention. They work as an ensemble with the exterior spaces, unlike a lot of modern architecture that tends to be designed as free-standing objects rather than as a backdrop. Here, the spatial composition relies on symmetry – apart from the bell tower and the off-centre cedar tree in the central green.

The buildings follow a strict module and have a clarity of repetition. There's the danger that this might be boring but it certainly isn't. The façade of each building is closed off in a different way – one is clad all the way down, one is open with a brise-soleil, another closed with brick. It's very Miesian but with a Scandinavian sensibility.

There is a real craftsmanship in Jacobsen's architecture which we revel in and aspire to, a finesse in details that takes ages to work out well. Nowadays, there seems to be a polarisation between fine art and craft in architecture, but the craft element – really understanding how you make a building – should be considered far more.

With a bit of experience as an architect, you realise that each job probably has one killer detail that defines the quality of the whole, and in this case it's the relationship between column, beam, glazing and roof. Here, an architect at the peak of his powers has had the foresight to work out and really craft these details. Each component has complete clarity, which gives each major room or assembly an integrity that is sadly lacking in so much current skin-deep architecture.

Jacobsen was a regionalist. He was clearly aware of Oxford's traditional quad colleges and very keen to absorb that in his design – he asked for plans of all the colleges to be sent over to Copenhagen when he was designing it. What's particularly inventive is how the rigid formality begins to break down as you move out at the ends. The main quad space turns into a sequence of gardens enclosed by freestanding masonry walls infilled with hedges of yew trees, implying a cloister.

This is my favourite part of the whole college. The door to the senior common rooms is a panel of wood with glass panes on either side. This matches the size of the canopy that cantilevers from the walls. The design isn't purely functional. Jacobsen kept the canopy away from the edges of the walkway. Everything is so light. It's sublime. It's an architectural landscape completely supportive of the building.

The integrity of the architecture runs throughout all the buildings. Everything is so complete, right down to the tapestry and the furniture, ceramics and cutlery in the dining room, which he designed as well. It is patronage of the highest order, not only commissioning it, but looking after it so well for 50 years.

Denise Bennetts

St Catherine's was the first new-build college in Oxford for centuries. Even now, it's the only college campus that isn't closed off at night. It isn't a contained quad. The whole Jacobsen grid loosens and fragments towards the margins. He gets around a lot of the problems of traditional quads – such as how you go around the corner – by having these separate elements of building and landscape. This integration of landscape is quite three-dimensional, with external rooms formed with yew hedges.

It's fascinating to see photographs from the sixties of the canopy with the tiny yew trees before they've grown. He had the vision for what it would be like in years to come whereas nowadays, mature trees would be brought in. There is something satisfying about a building maturing and growing rather than springing up fully formed.

Jacobsen shows that geometric repetition is no enemy to creating a sensitive building. Instead, it can be a mechanism for orchestrating things in a poetic way. At St Catherine's' there is a real clarity of construction, with a simple articulation of frame and infill, with every element acknowledging the presence of its partners. The language of Jacobsen's architecture has a sense of buildability about it, which we like.

Jacobsen taught us how to look at the details, which are here infused with the character of the materials. The brickwork is wonderful. He wanted to use a lighter coloured brick that would reflect the light more but there was uncertainty over whether the order could be met, so in the end he used a British brick but with reduced height to mimic the proportions of Continental bricks. Everything was designed to the brick module so there are no odd cut bricks anywhere.

Jacobsen took everything down to the last detail, playing with the same few materials to create different effects in each space, whether in the exceptional volume of the dining hall or the smaller common rooms. In the senior common room, for example, everything is more intimate with elements of asymmetry in particular spaces to define where principal activities are to take place. These subliminal messages are still being heeded and are preferable to the story that Jacobsen wanted some carpets woven with dots to show where to position chairs.

Despite the size of the building, it has a wonderful domestic scale both inside and out. I think one of the best ways to appreciate it is to study the ground plan with the buildings and the landscape determined by the same 3 metre grid. It results in an intensity of internal and external spaces but always with the respite of the open aspect to the south and north.

Above: The dining hall. Architect Arne Jacobsen was responsible for all aspects of the college's design from architecture to cutlery.

Far left: View towards the entrance to the senior common room. This cloister-like space is formed by yew hedges and is one of Rab Bennetts' favourite parts of the college.

Left: Detail of table lights in the main dining hall.

GREAT DANE Founded in 1962, St Catherine's is Oxford's youngest and largest college. It caused a stir when it appointed Arne Jacobsen, a Dane, to design its buildings rather than a British architect, but the decision was a success. Nikolaus Pevsner referred to it as "the perfect piece of architecture" while Reyner Banham approvingly called it "the best motel in Oxford".

Built on a marshy site on the outskirts of the city centre, the college consists of two parallel, three-storey residential blocks with covered arcades plus four separate blocks containing common rooms, dining hall, library and lecture rooms running north to south between them. There is also a master's house on the other side of a river, and a separate music room.

In 1993, the college was one of the first post-war buildings to be given Grade I listed status. Additional residential accommodation designed by Stephen Hodder was completed in 1994 and 2005.

The Cripps Building, St John's College

Location: Cambridge, UK
Architect: Powell & Moya
Completed: 1966–67
Chosen by Alun Jones and Biba Dow of Dow Jones Architects

Alun Jones (left) and Biba Dow (right) on the roof of The Cripps Building, a student residence at St John's College, Cambridge.

Alun Jones

I first got to know the Cripps building in 1990 when I came up to Cambridge to study for my diploma.

You approach it through an enfilade of urban rooms that form the first three courts of the college, cross the river by the Bridge of Sighs, and then turn through New Court, a slightly sterile nineteenth-century gothic heap. Passing through a narrow passage in the centre of New Court you burst out into a garden space and there's the Powell & Moya building, gleaming white and modern, basking in the sun. The juxtaposition is really extraordinary.

At the time, not a lot of people at Cambridge were interested in modernism, and I am sure a lot of my contemporaries would have seen this building as a bit of sub-Corb modernism, but it's anything but that. I remember at the time thinking it was a really interesting building but the quality and subtlety of the building is more apparent to me now. Over the last 15 years I've brought a lot of students here. I think it is a really good lesson in form and space making. It is also a lesson in looking beyond what something looks like and into that which it really is. After all, it isn't fashionable to like 1960s English modernism.

The thing I find most interesting is the plan configuration. The building is very long and narrow, and snakes through the college grounds, creating a number of spaces between itself and the existing college buildings. The way it engages with the site and makes sense of all the disparate organisation of buildings around it is brilliant. It forms several courtyards with these buildings, negotiating an inlet of the Cam, the back of New Court and the

School of Pythagoras, making a sequence of four courtyards even though it's not itself a courtyard building.

Most modernist buildings were very much object buildings. But this has an inherent modesty and is quite recessive – the spaces between itself and the other buildings are more important than the building itself. It's really very generous.

When you look at the building more closely, it's clear that Powell & Moya was engaging with the cloister typology, what Oxbridge colleges are, and how these analogous elements could be reworked on this site.

The building has really quite an emphatic horizontality that is broken up by the staircases and their penetration through the roof plane. These staircases are completely open at ground-floor level. As you climb, you end up inside the stone and glass rooftop pavilion, but you're never quite inside the building. It is a curious inside-outside experience. The roof used to be covered with students revising, drinking beer, playing chess, having parties – it was like a village. Unfortunately it's now shut to student access.

There's a lot of subtlety and variety with how the building meets the ground. Near the river, for example, the Portland stone used at ground-floor level is very shelly and aqueous and the building is more solid. As you move away from the river the building becomes more open at the ground floor and the landscape flows through the cloister.

The colleges are such fantastic patrons because they are very ambitious. Sometimes, as with the Cripps Building at St John's, they get it right.

Biba Dow

I first got to know the Cripps Building when I was an architecture student at Cambridge, visiting my cousin who lived in the building for two years. I do really like it. It's a quiet, confident building – quite mute, yet quite rich. As a student, it's probably not the sort of building that'll really rock your boat but I think you appreciate its subtleties as you learn more about making buildings.

It's on a beautiful site where the formality of the principal college buildings on the east side of the river gives way to the open space of the Backs on the west bank. The Cripps building combines the formality of the reinterpreted college cloister with the informality of the backs of buildings found along the river.

The stairways dropping down into the Cripps cloister, taking you up to the student rooms, seem to me to have the informality and light

touch of the steps found all along the riverbank where buildings back onto the river.

I worked at Powell & Moya before starting our practice and I remember Jacko Moya's full-size details of the ironmongery for Cripps.

There are various window and door catches and latches, cupboard door knobs and hooks in the bedrooms, as well as one-off items like the beautiful opening panel with a bronze latch in the porter's lodge window. This was all designed specially for the building and one of the delights when we re-visited it was seeing and using them.

The building uses few materials — Portland stone, pre-cast concrete, lead cladding and glass externally; and internally, hardwood and bronze with plastered walls and ceilings. This limited palette makes you very aware of place and the relationship between the building and the site context.

As a practice, Dow Jones is interested in a limited, restrained palette, which is worked in different ways. At Poplar Cottage in Walberswick, we only used clay and oak, finding many different ways with only two materials. At Lant Street in Bermondsey we built a glass and oak roofscape of interconnecting garden spaces on top of an old Victorian factory. At the time we thought of it as being like Robert Smythson's sweetmeat pavilions at Longleat stately home in Wiltshire, but coming here now, we see a more contemporary, or even subliminal analogy with the Cripps Building.

We've been involved in a number of contemporary interventions in historic buildings. In these situations, the threshold between old and new, and finding appropriate analogies to work with, seem to us to be the key. Powell & Moya did that very successfully here, and have made an utterly contemporary building that is embedded in the culture of the college.

Above: The building has a limited external palette of Portland stone, concrete, lead cladding and glass. Its strong horizontality is broken up by the staircases and their penetration into the roof plane.

Above, far left: The Cripps Building backs onto the River Cam and has a zigzag form that creates two new courts.

Above left: One of the many bespoke bronze ironmongery details found throughout the Cripps Building.

BRONZE BEAUTY Built to help meet post-war student expansion, the Cripps Building at St John's College was paid for by the Cripps Foundation. The Cripps family owned a piano factory that used bronze for the strings, and this perhaps helps explain the particularly large amount of bronze detailing inside this building.

The building zigzags through the site from the Cam to create two new courts – River Court in conjunction with the New Court building and Merton in conjunction with the School of Pythagoras, along the way reconciling any awkward changes in angle. It rises four storeys above ground-floor cloisters, allowing views to the river and the 'Backs', an area where several colleges back onto the River Cam. It is topped by an extensive roof terrace with concrete benches forming a parapet. Rooms are arranged around eight staircases. Most are divided by a sliding partition that separates the bed and sink from the study area. There are 12 duplex penthouse studios.

The Cripps building is now Grade II* listed.

Peter Barber revisits the "very moving" Faculty of Architecture at the University of Porto.

Faculty Of Architecture, University Of Porto

Location: Porto, Portugal
Architect: Álvaro Siza
Completed: 1987–93
Chosen by Peter Barber of Peter Barber Architects

I first heard about Álvaro Siza when I was studying for my diploma at the Polytechnic of Central London. When I finally saw Siza's work for myself it was a shock, completely alien to the hi-tech seventies and eighties stuff in England. There everything was about articulated structure and niftily detailed cladding systems, but Siza turns his structure into sculpture. His architecture seemed to be about concealment, seduction and poetry. He wanted to hide the technological and instead articulate pure form and space.

I'd been immersed in a functionalist environment for my first degree in Sheffield. I loved Archigram and had come to PCL to study under David Greene, and when I left I was interested in the idea of an architecture of ephemerality and lightness. My encounters with the work of Siza and also Luis Barragán while I was working for Richard Rogers made me look at architecture in a different way – the idea of mass and solidness – architecture embedded physically, culturally, geometrically in a particular site.

Having already seen other Siza buildings in Porto such as his wonderful salt-water swimming pool and the Boa Nova tearooms, I visited the Faculty of Architecture in 1994 not long after it had opened. I'd never seen anything like it. Until then, the buildings I'd adored had been very different – more mechanistic – gadgetry, dominated by structure. Through Siza I came to enjoy buildings that are more enigmatic.

I found the Porto University buildings very moving. You feel as if the architect is speaking to you and exerting a subtle but profound influence as you walk around, as if his hand is in the small of your back coaxing you gently through as the spaces unfold in picturesque sequence. It's a building you discover gradually. As I've come back five or six times over the years the subtleties of the building have slowly dawned on me as I've become more familiar with it. It's so different to Rem Koolhaas's recently completed Casa da Musica in Porto which looks as if it's crash landed from outer space. That is much more instantly understood than Siza's work, which is more layered, complex, nuanced and locally embedded.

Siza is very quiet and self-assured and this building also has a quiet confidence about it, a subtlety that makes people look at it more carefully. When you walk into the central space, your pace quickens because it arouses your curiosity and you want to discover it. For me that is what is magical about architecture. I like architecture that throws curve balls – you think it'll be one thing and it turns out to be something else. And there's a lot happening – it looked like Siza pored over joints and junctions for days to get them right. One of my favourites is an informal meeting place or hallway below the fifth-year tower, the building's principal point of circulation where numerous routes and axes converge and settle into a space teeming with people rushing through, stopping for a chat, sitting down for a cuppa. As such, it has an urban quality that I like. The arrangement of the buildings around a central square makes the faculty feel like a fragment of city.

Siza has said that architecture is meaningless until it is occupied, and it seems to me that he thinks profoundly about how his spaces will be used. On a busy day, the central space is brought to life by students playing football and sitting out on the strange truncated tower. My early encounters with his buildings helped me to think about architecture this way.

In the context of a lot of public and education sector architecture in England, the Porto architecture faculty shows us how to make a place that's calmly confident and lovingly made – civic and not corporate, unlike so many university buildings. I'd rather be here than in any other architecture school I've been in. But at the same time, is there a tyranny here in that students are in a Siza building and they're being taught in a Siza way?

When I visited the architecture faculty, it helped me consolidate my enthusiasm for an architecture of solidity, and my determination to work with mass and simple form. After working for Rogers and Alsop I set up my own practice and travelled to Saudi Arabia where I spent a year building my first project, Villa Anbar, which I think shows Siza's influence.

A lot of our work is about streets and public space, and I love the generosity of the Siza building. It is part of the city's public space and we are invited to walk through it. I like to think that my own urban housing projects are conceived in this spirit. Donnybrook and Tanner Street in east London and the project that predates them – a masterplan for Haggerston West and Kingsland estates in Hackney – are all conceived as pieces of city knitted into their surroundings.

The design of the Porto faculty is very knowing. It's redolent of the Porto streetscape and there are shades of Loos, Aalto and Corb in it. Maybe it's an architects' architecture. The campus continues to fascinate me and I'm sure it won't be long before I'm back. But you have to keep moving on. I'm getting really interested in 'home made' self-build housing and I'm also fascinated by the tumultuous street life made possible by a really dense city like Marrakech.

Left: The library, positioned in the north wing of the faculty along with an auditorium, lecture halls and departmental offices.

Below: An underground walkway beneath the courtyard links all the faculty buildings.

A number of studio towers are arranged around a campus courtyard along with the north-wing faculty building. Peter Barber admires its civic rather than corporate character.

UNIVERSITY EDUCATION Álvaro Siza was an appropriate choice to create a new architecture faculty at Porto, having studied at the university before establishing his practice in the city in 1954.

Completed in 1993, the faculty covers 87,000sq m on a sloping site overlooking the Douro River. Siza conceived the accommodation as a single large-scale building with inner courtyard, but developed the design into a number of smaller, interlinked volumes. Teaching and architectural research takes place in a row of studio towers. Departmental offices, lecture halls, an auditorium and a library are arranged behind them within the north wing, which acts as an acoustic buffer to the busy road behind. On the top floor is the fifth year studio.

All four towers are linked at basement level by a generous corridor that converges with the basement circulation of the north wing. Above ground, a central meeting space is semi-enclosed between the north building and the towers.

Michál Cohen at the top of the grand staircase at Hellerup School in Copenhagen. This multi-functional atrium is surrounded by informal teaching spaces.

Hellerup School

Location: Copenhagen, Denmark
Architect: Arkitema
Completed: 2002
Chosen by Michál Cohen of Walters & Cohen Architects

Hellerup School is a one-off. It's not a pristine, perfect piece of architecture or landscape, but a brilliant interpretation of the brief – the first of a new type of open-plan school typology that I'm aware of. I visited the school on a study trip with the British Council for School Environments in about 2006. The head teacher showed us around, and it blew me away.

The school is so different from anything you'll find in the UK; it was as if someone had taken the blinkers off, and it made me wish I could go back to school. I realised that the school vision, curriculum and pedagogy are essential to the design of a school. If educators want to encourage independent learners, then architects can point to buildings like Hellerup that are so interactive and flexible.

Hellerup School provides pupils and teachers with an environment that encourages personalised learning. The outside is very unadorned, but in a good way. The 'wow' factor is inside, which has a very different sensibility. When you enter, the big atrium space overwhelms you. It's completely open with small group break-in spaces, rather than separate classrooms with break-out spaces. Even the staff area is designed to be open to the rest of the school.

Hellerup is also very beautiful with a clean palette of render, timber and linoleum, and so is the quality of the light in the generous, top-lit central atrium. This impressive space gives focus to the entire school.

Hellerup has a very relaxed environment. The first time I visited, a class was sitting on the stairs having a lesson. We had our presentation in the auditorium, which is also a staircase, and pupils were walking up the side during the presentation, which wasn't a problem for anyone. This time, they've just been playing games at the top of the stairs. Others are on sofas or at computers. On the terrace a boy is preparing a barbecue. Lots of life skills are being taught, not just academic theory.

At first it looks messy, but when you analyse it, it's all organised. Leading off from the main space on three levels are areas that act as bases for each class, each with their own computers, toilets and kitchen. There's no central dining room – each group prepares its own lunch and eats in its own space together.

Each base has mobile screens that can form a circular space where the whole class gathers first thing in the morning to talk about the day. They are then taught together or they find a suitable space where they can work in small groups or individually.

The absence of a formal timetable means that there are no bells, which contributes to the relaxed atmosphere. Instead, all pupils have their own timetable. Every space is flexible because of the mobile storage and screens, except for subjects like science, woodwork and cooking, which need special equipment.

Hellerup was revolutionary. It's not prissy, and stands up really well to its flexible use. And unlike in the UK, there's a very sensible approach to regulations. For example, at Hellerup, the toilets are individual cubicles directly off the main space (rather than behind an extra door) and that avoids any potential problem with bullying in the toilets.

When I visited the first time, up the stairs and just a metre or so away from the top there were pupils playing ping-pong and no-one was

saying they couldn't do that. Likewise there were some girls on very lofty swings in the gym. It's about helping children to judge risk.

Hellerup was one of the first open-style schools that everyone in the UK got excited about. When I saw the school published in 2003, the way it dealt with the lack of formal teaching spaces was very innovative.

These ideas aren't entirely new: there were a lot of open-plan schools in the UK in the 1970s, but often the spaces were too small and they didn't have the right acoustics, so the idea failed. At Hellerup, however, the spaces are generous and all ceilings and balustrades have acoustic absorption.

The size of school has a lot to do with its success – there are only 400 or so pupils so it is very personal in scale. The architects also had the luxury of six months at feasibility level talking about what might work without putting pen to paper compared with our 14 weeks of design under the Academies Framework before putting in for planning. Another factor was that the school didn't occupy it for at least six months, allowing educationalists and staff to try out furniture and layouts.

Many UK architects have been inspired by elements of Hellerup's design, especially the stairs. Hellerup allowed us to consolidate some of our ideas. For example, we had been thinking that it would be good not to centralise the

toilets and we took heart from how this had worked so well at Hellerup. We also realised that it was possible to get the acoustics right in big spaces without having to shut them off.

We speak to head teachers constantly about some of the ideas we see at Hellerup and at other inspirational schools. However, I don't think we'll ever have a UK school where pupils are trusted in the same way, with the same approach to the curriculum and pedagogy.

Apparently Hellerup's first year was difficult as staff and pupils adjusted to such a different school environment, but it has since become a top performing school. There's a happiness there. And happy children learn.

Above left: Hellerup's generous main staircase, which is variously used for circulation, teaching and seating, has proved highly influential on school design elsewhere.

Above right: The central 'heart' space at the foot of the main staircase can accommodate various functions including library space.

Opposite: The simple, unadorned exterior contains a variety of learning spaces with an emphasis on openness and flexibility of usage.

INNOVATIVE LEARNING Hellerup School, situated in north Copenhagen, teaches six to 16 year olds. Designed by architects Arkitema, the 8200sqm school is arranged around a wide stepped area within a generous atrium, which forms a multi-purpose 'heart' space.

The school pioneered a flexible approach to learning environments, with easily re-configured space and a choice of settings. The atmosphere is relaxed – all pupils, staff and visitors remove their outdoor shoes on arrival – and there are no formal school perimeter boundaries.

Cultural Buildings

EXHIBITION PIECE Mies van der Rohe designed the German National Pavilion to host the official German reception for the 1929 Barcelona International Exhibition, held in the Montjuïc district of the city. The steel-framed structure was built using four different kinds of stone – Roman travertine, green Alpine marble, green Greek marble and golden onyx from the Atlas mountains.

Mies, who worked on the interior of the pavilion with designer Lilly Reich, created his famous Barcelona chair for the building. The pavilion was dismantled in 1930 but continued to be a key point of reference as a symbol of modernism.

Fifty years later, Barcelona City Council commissioned architects Ignasi de Solà-Morales, Cristian Cirici and Fernando Ramos to research and reconstruct the building, and in 1986 the building opened on its original site. It is now home to the Fundació Mies van der Rohe, which was set up by the City to organise the reconstruction of the pavilion and to promote knowledge of Mies and his work.

Inside the Barcelona Pavilion, which was rebuilt in 1986. The interior is dominated by an onyx marble wall. The glazed rear elevation opens onto a small courtyard and pool.

Barcelona Pavilion

Location: Barcelona
Architect: Ludwig Mies van der Rohe
Completed: 1929 (rebuilt 1986)
Chosen by Keith Williams of Keith Williams Architects

Some of the most influential projects ever made were ephemeral, enduring only in grainy photographs like some beautiful film star who died too young. Yet such projects have nonetheless had a fundamental effect on the direction of architecture.

Mies' German Pavilion was designed for the Barcelona International Exhibition of 1929, and was demolished the following year. As a student, I pored over its diagrammatic plans and the few grainy photos of the building, delighting in an imagined journey through its sparse, labyrinthine but exquisitely conceived plan, and the engagement with its austere horizontality.

This work by one of the twentieth century's greatest architects redefined our notions of surface, space and architecture, and I never imagined that I would see it. Why would I? It had after all only existed for less than a year during Mies' own lifetime. Yet it was improbably brought back to life when reconstructed between 1983 and 1986. We do not know in absolute terms how faithful this facsimile was to the original, but I think it is pretty close.

I first visited in 1991 and everything immediately seemed to me familiar. The stunning interplay of both wall surface and ground plane; the improbably thin horizontality of the roof sailing across the walls seemingly unconstrained by normal limits; and the skin of the surface of the pool in the terrace seeming taut and unruffled.

I was enthralled by the theatrically orchestrated vistas; the transparency and the layering of space playing tricks with one's reading of spatial depth; the way daylight illuminates the surfaces of stone and water; and the super shiny cruciform columns in stainless steel, so thin that they appear almost to be in tension. Alba,

a sculpture by Georg Kolbe placed within a top-lit pool deep in the labyrinth, forms a single focal point. The huge, stone wall slabs are truly heroic in scale yet the proportional ratio of 2:1 that unites them with the smaller square grid of the ground surfaces is effortlessly pleasing. Somehow, it all maintains a connection with the human dimension.

What I could never understand from the drawings and photos was the exquisite character of the materials: the sumptuous richness of grained colour of the dark marble walls, the travertine floor slabs, and the translucency of the book-matched golden onyx wall panels. There is a strange desire to run one's fingertips across its surfaces rather as though stroking the bodywork of a fabulously expensive new car.

The beautifully ordered and richly layered plan was never intended to have much in it, offering little more than tranquillity amid the hubbub of an international fair. And to accompany this building, Mies also gave us the Barcelona chair.

Designed when he was already in his mid 40s, the pavilion was still a test-bed where Mies honed the rules that would govern much of his later work. The pavilion was contemporary with Villa Tugendhat in Brno, which shares aspects of similar detailing and materiality but was comparatively constrained by the functional programme of the home. With the German Pavilion, however, Mies could give free rein to spatial exploration.

Mies' fundamental contribution to architecture was cemented in later years through far larger and more expansive buildings. But I would suggest that Mies never bettered this, his temporary masterpiece, which more than 80 years later still stirs the spirit.

Hans van der Heijden in the small, chapel-like sculpture gallery at the Museum Boijmans van Beuningen.

Museum Boijmans Van Beuningen

Location: Rotterdam, Netherlands
Architect: Adrianus van der Steur
Completed: 1928–35
Chosen by Hans van der Heijden

My fascination with the Boijmans has everything to do with the evolution of my own architectural thinking.

This building is a very important art museum, so I knew it first from going to exhibitions when I was studying in Delft, which is quite near Rotterdam. Because it was the 1980s, modernism was dominant and we were all designing white boxes. As a result, I wasn't really all that taken by the Boijmans building. My real fascination with it came later when I was working at Mecanoo, where the architects were real white box babies. They imposed an architecture on the site that was technically very difficult and we were battling constantly with contractors to get it right. I began to feel dissatisfied with this approach.

I come from a building family – my grandfather was a carpenter, my father an architectural technician, and their view was that a building should be the product of a collaborative construction team – a very different view to that of the Mecanoo world. I started looking beyond modernism. In Rotterdam, I found a collection of buildings, including the Boijmans museum, that were made of brick and although these were not consistent in style, they were all self-consciously public buildings. They were communicating in a very acceptable, low-key way with bricks, plaster and stone. They don't shout. They are extremely civilised. I like that a lot.

Back at Mecanoo, I showed my slides of the Italian buildings I admired to colleagues and they were, of course, appalled. I had learned a lot at Mecanoo – it was very dynamic – but I now knew precisely what I didn't want, and it was necessary to start an office with like-minded colleagues to run our own programme.

Buildings that are the product of Rotterdam's economic expansion have been forgotten. Before its destruction by the Luftwaffe in 1940, Rotterdam must have had a rich urban image. That has gone. Post-war reconstruction was an economic affair, ruthlessly executed by a second generation of modernists. Even today, brick buildings like the Boijmans aren't really recognised as architecturally important and have been excluded from the design canon. But they could be a very good antidote to the self-image that Rotterdam cherishes: of itself as a city in a constant state of renewal. But its traditional port activity is no longer happening in the city centre, and the issue now is how to reinvent those parts of Rotterdam for more domestic use.

The Rotterdam city architect Adrianus van der Steur, designed the Boijmans and the garden and the interior as one, which gives it a great coherence. To me, it seems that although people might not be that aware of the beauty of the architecture, they do accept the place as somewhere familiar and pleasant.

When it was built in the 1930s, the Boijmans was the most modern museum in Europe. During the design process, the client and architect took a tour of the 20 best museums in Europe and as part of the research, they built full-scale mock-ups of roof-lit galleries to test the light and shadows. Only the ground floor, where the galleries were made to display crafts and design, has windows – the upper floors have rooflights to create the right light conditions for the paintings.

Technically, the building had all the state-of-the-art novelties, including air conditioning. Amazingly, it took just four years to conceive and construct the entire edifice.

The building has the ethos of being traditional in a modern context. For a big institutional building, it doesn't have a really monumental appearance, but uses brick as an expressive material. In essence, it's a brick shed with a bell tower. At first glance you think it's quite a harsh building, but its nuance is in the details. Modernism has difficulty with what I call the zoom factor – close by, a white box looks the same as it does from afar. But this building is like a painting. As you get closer, you see more details. It's quite delicate.

The original main entrance is really special. There's this classical way of how you develop an entrance using a small space, then a bigger space, then an even bigger space, while developing the spaces off to the side. The biggest space is an oval rather than a circle, and suddenly there's a green floor and a black plinth, a linguistic turn that you don't find anywhere else in the building, yet here it makes sense.

Inside, everything is very axial and incredibly detailed. The building does not want to be ostentatiously precious. Yet, everything is considered – not necessarily by the architect alone, but also by those actually putting the building together. In the galleries that are designed for sculpture there are stone plinths, but in the rooms where paintings are shown, the plinths are wood.

What's also interesting is how the rooms connect – the design is very much about how you navigate through the space. You move from room to room – there are no corridors or fluid spaces. I particularly love how the curved seating is incorporated into the wall of the galleries along the circulation route through these enfilade rooms – the result is

beyond beautiful and is a baroque twist on the otherwise axial space.

I took our Bluecoat Arts Centre clients here when we were designing their extension in Liverpool, and they appreciated how there was a great intensity to the spaces, and they were also taken by the use of brick as an architectural material. I learned at the Bluecoat how difficult it is to design circulation around a wing. Here, van der Steur was very clever to add a small chapel-like space for sculpture at the end of the wing to connect the two end galleries. From a theoretical point of view, it's a classical building. Classicism is often dismissed as a closed system that excludes the imagination of its author, but this is full-on imaginative.

Today, I still go to visit the Boijmans quite often. It's a building in which you can wander around and see different things in the architecture every time, and there are very few buildings in which you can do that.

View through the enfilade galleries showing the built-in seating at the entrance to each space. The effect, says Hans van der Heijden, is "beyond beautiful."

CIVIC EXAMPLE Adrianus van der Steur (1893–1953) was municipal architect of Rotterdam and was commissioned to design a new building and park for the Boijmans Van Beuningen Museum. Founded in 1849, this gallery is today particularly known for its surrealist collection.

Van der Steur, together with the municipal urban designer WG Witteveen, envisaged a city of solid brick and stone buildings forming classical streets and squares. They clad the building in red brick and included a stately tower, which was illuminated at night. Inspired by the domestic interiors of private collectors, Boijmans contained a series of small-scale galleries with subtle detailing.

The museum survived the bombing in 1940 that destroyed much of the city centre. Originally arranged around two courtyards, the building has since been expanded several times, most notably by a new wing for temporary exhibitions by Alexander Bodon (1972) and a pavilion designed by Hubert-Jan Henket (1991), which greatly altered the building's relationship with the landscape. Originally designed as a gallery, this extension is now used as a restaurant. An extension by Robbrecht & Daem (2001) to the Bodon building includes new galleries and a library.

The Boijmans museum is one of a series of low-key, brick civic buildings in Rotterdam from the 1930s. Later additions include a pavilion overlooking the surrounding park landscape.

Paul Williams with the Cangrande I statue at the 'wonderfully orchestrated' Castelvecchio Museum in Verona.

Castelvecchio Museum

Location: Verona, Italy
Architect: Carlo Scarpa (restoration)
Completed: 1958–64
Chosen by Paul Williams of Stanton Williams

For me, Castelvecchio offers wholeness. It's not simply a restored building with works of art in it, it's an ensemble with everything worked out. Many buildings move me, but none quite like this. When I go around it, I find myself smiling because I know where Carlo Scarpa is coming from, his thought process, his passions. It's as if I am in a silent dialogue with him.

I first saw images of Scarpa's work when I was a student in the early 1970s. I remember my jaw dropping. The images were a revelation, with art being displayed in such a considered and sensitive way. It showed an approach to restoration integrating new and old that was so in advance of anything I had seen before. This was, of course, well before Scarpa's work gained a reputation in the UK. I visited Castelvecchio and also his Brion Cemetery soon afterwards, and I have no doubt that what I encountered then was what led me into exhibition design.

Scarpa unpicked a cruder 1920s restoration, stripping back inappropriate layers to expose more of the historic fortifications, then modifying his designs to accommodate the most interesting finds. Throughout, Scarpa managed to maintain both a mental and visual clarity to create one of the finest examples of how to juxtapose old and new, creating something greater than the sum of its parts.

At Castelvecchio, you're taken on a wonderful orchestrated journey from the minute you go through the courtyard, walking on the Prun stone that is all over Verona, then through into the galleries and up and onto the battlements. It is a very sensory experience. Castelvecchio seems to encapsulate all the knowledge Scarpa had learnt over many years, born out of a commitment to rigorous craftsmanship and a minimalistic aesthetic.

His thought processes were complex, although the results are invariably simple. Where any element, material or surface came close to or engaged with another, there needed to be a response, a thickening or thinning, a texture change or smoothing, an understanding of which element is in the ascendancy.

He never complicated details by trying to do two things at once – instead he completed a move then started another. There is never any confusion between past and present. He allowed the historic building to breathe and be understood. In my mind no other architect has done that in quite the same way.

Scarpa obviously spent a great deal of time assessing the architectural dynamics of a space and its exhibits. Each work of art is displayed with nuance and sensitivity. The design was continually aiming to create a very private experience between viewer and object, where the object is offered up as if in an outstretched hand, to facilitate an interaction.

In the ground-floor sculpture galleries he created a five-room enfilade, drawing visitors through each opening with the use of large, thick, textured slabs of stone that clad the archways to create a more human scale to the dimensions of the passageway, matched to the spring line of the arches.

Everything is considered. In each of the slightly asymmetric galleries, he has pulled the floor away from the wall to set up his own geometrical grid and used alternating bands of concrete and stone, set at various widths to suit the displays. As horizontals, running across the gallery floor, they intentionally slow you down on your way through, and set up a new controlled dynamic.

The sacellum, which protrudes from slightly inside the gallery into the courtyard, clearly reads as a new intervention and feels like stepping into a polished plaster box, with a rich red flooring used to suit the more intimate dimensions of the space. In the next gallery, he breaks the clear view through the enfilade with one figure, which he brings forward. The statues are positioned to face away from each other, encouraging the visitor to move around to confront every piece head-on.

This richness of detail came out of his understanding of the specifics of each display situation, and his respect for the history of the building and its contents. In the fourth sculpture gallery, for example, he displayed the crucifixion group by the Master of Sant'Anastasia with two figures on either side of the statue of Christ on a metal backdrop that we read as a cross. He took just a little notch out of the top of the metal 'T', which

was enough to turn it from a T into the crucifix. What's beautiful is the way the two other pieces inhabit the voids of the cross on either side.

The desire for clarity and honesty is apparent everywhere. Where there is a new surface, for example, on the steps at the end of the ground floor galleries, he revealed the bricks underneath so that we read the stone as a new layer. Where there is a false wall he lifts it off the ground to show that it isn't self-supporting or load-bearing. Some might say that this degree of nuance and refinement is at times too fussy. Perhaps yes, but for me, this is the work of a man at the full height of his powers. The setting created for the Cangrande I equestrian statue is one of Scarpa's greatest achievements. He bravely stripped back the original external skin of the barracks and exposed the interior structure to the elements. It's as if the innards of the building have broken out to form an external plinth for the statue. Upstairs in the

painting rooms, Scarpa intentionally ignored the walls and displayed works on freestanding easels. It's a very intimate encounter with each piece.

After visiting all great buildings, you know when they've touched you, but not always why. With Castelvecchio, I felt I knew why on my first visit, and Scarpa's approach has influenced my work ever since. Even today, when I come across an architectural problem, I invariably think about how he might tackle it. So powerful, and yet so calm and contemplative, this place is a sanctuary – everything a museum and gallery should be in this rather frenetic world we live in.

Above: The courtyard at Castelvecchio, which dates from the fourteenth century and was restored by Carlo Scarpa from 1958–64.

Right: Clad in squares of Prun stone, the sacellum protrudes through the courtyard façade. The intervention was part of Carlo Scarpa's renovations.

Detail of display fitting. Scarpa paid great attention to how every object was displayed, making new interventions clear.

EXEMPLARY RENOVATION Castelvecchio is part of the fourteenth century castle of Verona on the bank of the River Adige. The former barracks was restored in 1924-6 under the Fascist regime and reopened as a museum housing paintings, sculpture and other art works. It was damaged during the Second World War and renovated from 1958–64 by the Venetian architect Carlo Scarpa (1906–78), who specialised in museum refurbishment.

He developed a methodology in which he identified and removed any arbitrary additions and where possible revealed the original structure and successive layers of intervention, including his own. Scarpa devised a specific route for visitors through the museum that took them both inside and out, in the process giving different views of one of the museum's most important works, the equestrian statue of Cangrande I. Sculpture galleries are on the ground floor, with painting galleries on the upper levels. Restoration continued in several phases with the sentry walkways reopened in 2007.

View through the enfilade sculpture galleries on the ground floor. Scarpa deliberately broke the clear view by bringing one display plinth forward.

Paintings are displayed on easels in the upper galleries. The design is intended to encourage a more personal interaction with the exhibits.

James Soane outside the
"brutal yet sensuous" extension
to the Liverpool Playhouse
theatre, the building that
made him aware of modern
architecture.

Liverpool Playhouse Extension

Location: Liverpool, UK

Architect: Ken Martin of Hall O'Donahue & Wilson

Completed: 1968

Chosen by James Soane of Project Orange

The Liverpool Playhouse extension was conceived in the same year as me (1966) and every day at home I saw a photo of it from when it was newly completed, hanging on the wall of my father's study – he was a structural engineer and it was his first project. It entered into my consciousness before I even knew what architecture was.

We lived nearby in the Wirral. I remember going to the Playhouse when I was a kid and thinking it was so modern. It was a total environment with its glamorous restaurant, wire frame chairs and bright colours – I recall pinks and purples. I remember feeling the impact of something new and different as I went up this whizzy circulation space and then had the contrast of going through into the old auditorium. The first show I saw there was *Godspell* in 1978 – I've still got the programme.

It was built in the late sixties when Liverpool had a real buzz about it. There was all this regeneration happening before things started to go wrong for the city in the seventies. The extension isn't a famous building but buildings don't always have to be virtuoso performances. Instead, it was there to support the progressive theatre. However it was unusual and, I think, exceptional - a real bit of contemporariness in the city. It's neither replica nor pastiche but instead represents a completely different mood of architecture to the original theatre. I applaud the confidence that the building shows.

Whether you like it or not, the extension is still a very strong statement. It's kind of brutal yet sensuous. It's not trying to be politely modernist. At night, the transparency really comes into its own and you can see people milling about inside, eating and drinking. The extension was handmade in a fairly traditional

way. It's a prototype and belongs here in this context, and that comes across.

The Playhouse extension was the building that made me aware of modern architecture before I knew anything about it. It was experimental, pushing the planning boundaries and pushing the structural design but all within a budget, and those are things we aspire to in our work at Project Orange.

The Playhouse extension is not the first building to use the circulation and the function of the building to dictate the form, but is a very vivid and dynamic example. It works on the urban level because you see people animating the edge of the square while from within, you come out of the 'black box' of the theatre into the city. In that sense, the presence of people provides both the spectacle and the audience – it is in the spirit of the theatre.

While the design for the Playhouse extension grew out of its function, it's about rather more than that. The willful composition derived from the interrelationship of the three structural columns and the interior is spatially very rich. It also has a strong sense of the material – exposed concrete, glass, black-framed glazing etc, which made a very memorable interior at the time.

Coming back to visit the playhouse today, it's interesting to remember how pure the original was and to see how over time there's been this layering of bits and junk as well as cosmetic tweaks. But its sculptural design is so robust that it transcends this. It's powerful enough to take it. The space is fantastic and it still works well as a big window into the city, bulging out over the square. It's certainly still got something about it, and it wouldn't take much to put right.

SIXTIES SENSATION Designed by Ken Martin of Hall O'Donahue & Wilson, the dramatic extension in 1968 has been the most significant alteration to the Grade II* listed Liverpool Playhouse, which is the only surviving Victorian theatre still in active use in Merseyside.

The original theatre was designed by architect Edward Davies and completed in 1866 when it was known as the Star Music Hall. It became the home of the Liverpool Repertory Company in 1911. The 1968 extension was built to house a new entrance, box office bar and restaurant, which was later taken out.

The Playhouse closed in the late nineties and reopened in 2000 under the management of the Liverpool & Merseyside Theatres Trust, which also runs the city's Everyman Theatre.

Stephen Hodder outside the
Sainsbury Centre for the Visual
Arts in Norwich: "it challenged
everything I knew".

Sainsbury Centre for the Visual Arts, University of East Anglia

Location: Norwich, UK

Architect: Foster Associates

Completed: 1974–78

Chosen by Stephen Hodder of Hodder + Partners

There is a moment in an architect's life when they search for a certain direction and want to be uplifted and inspired. This is what the Sainsbury Centre did for me in 1978. At a time when people were rediscovering the values of context and tradition in architecture, this building restated some of the constants of architecture and showed that you can attain richness from just a simple idea. By rethinking the nature of gallery space, it reminded me of the great ability of modern architecture to continually reinvent itself.

I heard about the Sainsbury Centre in my third year at the Manchester School of Architecture when vernacular architecture was my main point of reference.

We each chose a building to analyse and one of my contemporaries chose the Sainsbury Centre, which had recently been completed. When I read his analysis, I struggled to understand how the building was able to contain both a gallery and a university department in a single space with seemingly no hierarchy to the circulation pattern. My curiosity was further aroused by an exhibition of the work of Foster Associates at the Whitworth Art Gallery in Manchester later that year.

I had to see it for myself. The following year I visited, entering at first-floor level through the Lasdun buildings via the linking walkway. The visit reinforced what I'd read. There is a great legibility to the building. As you walk down the spiral staircase you get a 360 degree view of the building, with alternating views of the lake and wood at either end. It's a great introduction to the building. Quite apart from the majesty of this incredible, light-filled space, there is an ethereal quality. I remember seeing a green glow and realising it was a reflection of the trees in the ceiling. Then, you start to appreciate the nuances: how the lines of the internal louvres along the side and in the ceiling give this incredible perspective that draws your attention to views at either end; how the steel-framed structure extends out beyond the building to blur the interior and exterior, and how you feel completely immersed among the artefacts in the gallery, despite its vastness.

I don't think of the Sainsbury Centre as a hi-tech building, although part of its significance was that there were so many technological firsts. It is a magical, beautiful space that is firmly grounded in the modern movement and not a building that's about an imposed style. The Pompidou Centre in Paris had been completed the previous year and it was the dawn of hi-tech.

Foster had recently completed the Fred Olsen Buildings [1969] and the Modern Art Glass factory [1973], and the Sainsbury Centre represented a culmination of this thinking. There was a concern for flexible space that would allow a building to change over its lifetime. The turning point for the design of this building was a sequence of decisions from the use of a clear-spanned space, to a solid frame and then to the use of triangular trusses of steel hollow sections that envelop a 2.4m-perimeter zone for the toilet pods and other 'servant' space, such as the air-handling units that sit on top of these pods.

Over the top of the whole thing are walkways and gantries for maintenance that could go on without affecting the main, 'served' space. This brilliant idea of maintaining all the services in the interstitial perimeter space allows natural top light to flood into the main space. Apparently, this idea of trapezoidal trusses and interstitial spaces was a last-minute change when the original tender drawings had already been completed.

The other striking thing was that the Sainsbury Centre was largely assembled rather than built. Above the undercroft, everything was pre-assembled. The frame came to site ready-finished and just had to be lifted into place and joined. By a good many years, it pre-empted the move towards prefabrication and dry construction. How appropriate that it was while visiting this building that Buckminster Fuller famously posed the question: "How much does your building weigh, Mr Foster?"

I also think the building pre-empted the whole concept of a team working together – there were intense collaborations with the structural engineer, Anthony Hunt, and other consultants such as the lighting designer.

The precision is quite extraordinary and made a huge impact on me as a student. I'd never seen structural glass balustrades before, nor that sort of unobtrusive glass hydraulic lift. At the time, the structural glass fins on the lakeside elevation were the largest ever produced. The original side panels were profiled silver, inspired apparently by the sides of a Citroën van. And the design of toilets is brilliant – apparently they were a reference to the cabins of a Boeing 747 aircraft.

The relationship Foster established with Lord and Lady Sainsbury was fundamental to the building's success. It was a remarkable client-architect relationship - they visited galleries together to work out what kind they wanted. The story is that Foster presented them with many options and Lady Sainsbury told him he should just do the one he wanted to do.

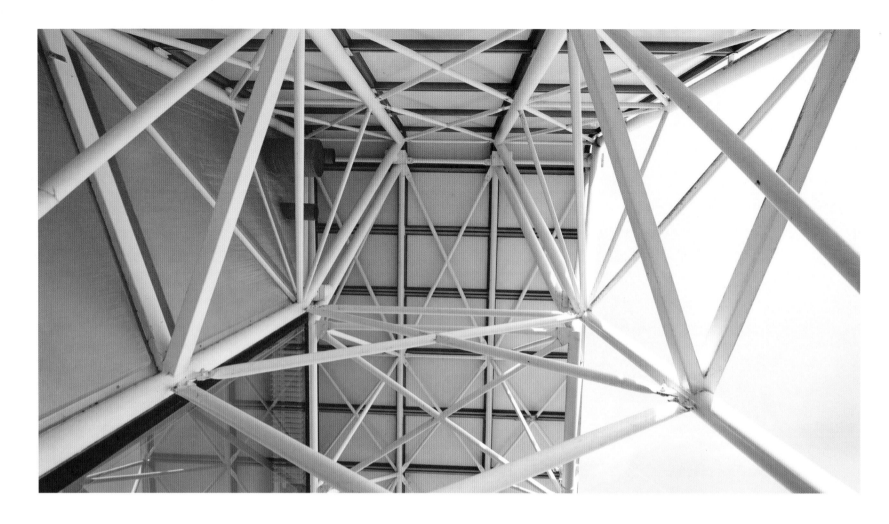

As you'd expect with a building as committed as this, it had mixed reviews at the time. It is a very particular response to the clients' wishes and challenged the fairly typical sequential gallery space model – there is an intimacy you can imagine the Sainsburys had in their own home. Yet there is a university department in there too, right next to the art collection, so that the students can mingle with the Giacomettis and Bacons.

For me, this experience was an awakening because it challenged everything I knew. At first, it very literally informed my own approach while working at BDP designing silver sheds for British Gas and also for British Nuclear Fuels at Sellafield.

After I set up my own firm, I started to distil the abstract qualities of the building – the form, the light, the technology, prefabrication and how it was conceived and put together.

After the 1979 visit, I hadn't been back until this revisit. The way the building was conceived and put together means it still has a freshness about it. It doesn't feel 33 years old and the 1991 extension is ingenious. However, the tremendous weeping figs that were originally near the entrance are a sad loss. The drawn blinds that are now pulled over the glazed lake elevation are also unfortunate since they make the building feel a little introspective. And the new white cladding gives a much crisper quality to the building than I remember the original having.

At the Sainsbury Centre, the practice was reinventing a building typology and at the same time creating an informative precursor to Stansted Airport. Reyner Banham actually described the centre as resembling an aircraft hangar but there is still an intimacy with the art, with the gallery re-creating the context of the collection in the Sainsburys' home.

The Sainsbury Centre's steel-framed design meant that the building was largely assembled rather than built on site, pre-empting the later move towards prefabrication and dry construction.

CHIC SHED Robert and Lisa Sainsbury commissioned Norman Foster to create a new home for their art collection after donating it to the University of East Anglia in 1973. The project was conceived as two separate buildings – one for the art collection and one for the university's facilities – but evolved into one large building containing both.

The building, which cost £4.2 million, was remarkable for its high proportion of off-site construction and for the arrangement of services within a 2.4m periphery to give a vast, unimpeded internal space – a last-minute design change.

Cracks started developing in the aluminium ribbed cladding panels by 1985 and were replaced in 1988 – this time with smooth white panels. Now Grade II * listed, the centre was extended in 1991 by the largely underground Crescent Wing, built with engineer Anthony Hunt Associates.

Service areas are pushed to the perimeter of the building to create a huge column-free space for the art collection. The perspective is emphasised by the ceiling design.

Roger Hawkins (left) and
Russell Brown (right)
outside the "intriguing and
sophisticated" Kunsthal gallery
in Rotterdam.

Kunsthal

Location: Rotterdam, Netherlands
Architect: OMA
Completed: 1987–92
Chosen by Russell Brown and Roger Hawkins of Hawkins/Brown

Russell Brown

When the Kunsthal was being built we saw Rem Koolhaas of OMA talk about it at the AA. We came out to see it together in 1993 and were so bowled over that we brought the whole Hawkins Brown studio out here in 2002.

The area around the Kunsthal is very busy nowadays but when we first came it had a bleak outlook and there was the sense that it was being built in frontier territory. Now the surrounding area feels very different, as if the building has civilised this part of Rotterdam.

The Kunsthal is known for its structural gymnastics and its very particular use of materials. It's not an expensive building, but Koolhaas shows that you can create big architecture with slim means. When he talked about it, Koolhaas gave the impression that the building was quite chaotic and full of compromise but really it isn't. Intriguing and sophisticated, it's witty without being a one-liner, knowing but naive, and human yet austere.

The plan is really hard-working with public movement through the centre along the ramp, while within the building there's private movement visible down a parallel ramp. The building questions what's inside and out, mirroring and contrasting movement but without wasting an inch of space.

Inside, the ramp continues steeply up through the auditorium or down to the café and exhibition hall. The nature of the ramp changes depending on the space – it's very rarely just used as circulation.

I love the auditorium with its different coloured chairs and the beautiful Petra Blaisse curtain, which can give more privacy while not interfering with circulation. It's a complex space that takes risks, superimposing circulation and occupied space. At the top, the ramp turns and continues upwards, while overflowing right into the auditorium. There's the sense that the rooms are never complete, with a complexity of levels and interpenetration of enticing views into different spaces.

On the south elevation, alongside the road, Koolhaas uses a range of different columns as if forming a catalogue of types of modernist column like the classical orders in a pattern book. It's a really complex architecture, and is a taste of what's to come inside. In the auditorium, there's a row of angled columns coming down the slope and you expect them to continue, but structurally they aren't needed so the row stops. Instead, suspended columns from the floor above protrude down into the space in the form of light fixtures.

In the main exhibition hall on the lower level Koolhaas uses hollowed-out trees to clad the steel stanchions – it's a surreal reference to the park outside. The building's structure appears almost as decoration or another level of expression. The ideas here are so strong, built into the fabric so that you can't value engineer them down. We feel jealous walking around. Rem must really be very persuasive. Clients in England just wouldn't trust you to do what he did with each elevation having a different glazing system and different materials.

Roger Hawkins

When I first saw the building I thought it was fantastic and I still do. I like architecture with wit and character and this is quite playful and full of surreal games.

It's a very simple plan divided off-centre into one large, one medium and two small spaces, with the tower to show you where the entrance is. There's a lot going on but somehow it all works together. It's very exciting, and it's clear that visitors really enjoy being in it.

Koolhaas spent more time designing the inside than the outside, and I don't think enough architects really do that. It's really considered, with a lot of attention given to the idea of promenade and the way the different parts of the building interrelate – there's the real impression that Koolhaas was creating a series of theatrical stage sets rather than a building. I've never seen such a steep sloping floor before – it must be 1:12 and health and safety officials would be horrified now, but here it really works. The design of the Kunsthal is also all about the internal quality – his use of daylight and attention to detail such as the balustrades, the wonderful curtain in the auditorium, the different types of columns. All are playing games with the space.

Koolhaas has been tremendously influential for us over the years. We like the way he talks about his buildings in relation to art, using his background as a filmmaker and a journalist. Like the Kunsthal, we think our Corby Cube civic centre seems bigger on the inside – it's a very simple plan but we've put a lot in there, using a ramp to promenade through the building and wrap around the spaces.

There's a temptation for a lot of buildings to apply cost indices evenly so that everything is dumbed down to a mid-range. But you don't have to be mediocre all the way through. Rem pushes the boundaries on the Kunsthal, using really expensive materials next to low-cost ones such as travertine alongside corrugated

plastic on the exterior. Our Dalston Culture House is almost a homage to a lot of this thinking. We used a similar plastic sheeting screening but in a finer grain.

The Kunsthal also shows that with a bit of thought, you can represent cheap materials as something more. In the New Art Exchange in Nottingham we borrowed the way the light fittings at the Kunsthal are embedded into the concrete soffit by recessing slots into the concrete ceiling, which meant we could use cheaper light fittings.

We often look to Koolhaas's work and Kunsthal in particular as a starting point in our work. It's such a clever ambitious building, one that really benefitted from being crafted over several years. We love it and we will keep coming back.

GALLERY GAMES The Kunsthal was one of OMA's first major built projects, completed in 1992 in collaboration with the structural engineer Cecil Balmond. The cultural centre provides 3,300sq m of exhibition spaces for temporary shows arranged over three halls and two galleries.

The 7,000sq m building is located along Rotterdam's busy Maasboulevard expressway on top of a dike, with the Museumpark neighbourhood to the north. A pedestrian ramp slopes down through the building from south to north while a road runs east/west beneath it at the top of the site.

Its square plan is divided into four parts connected by a continuous, spiralling route through the levels which creates views up, down, across and out as required, sometimes framing views of the park, sometimes offering glimpses of other levels. The building is full of surprises and inconsistencies. There is no single clear main elevation and each receives completely different treatments.

Russell Curtis (left), Dieter
Kleiner (centre) and Tim Riley
(right) in one of the ground-
floor galleries at the Palais de
Tokyo in Paris.

Palais De Tokyo

Location: Paris, France
Architect: Lacaton & Vassal
Completed: 2002 (further phase completed 2012)
Chosen by Russell Curtis, Dieter Kleiner and Tim Riley of RCKa

Dieter Kleiner

Palais de Tokyo is remarkable on a number of levels. It is a permanently temporary, non-institutional institution, with vast formal spaces rendered informal by the naked exposure of its elegant concrete frame.

The antithesis of monumental architecture, it subverts its grand art-deco host building to reveal failings and idiosyncrasies that give it personality and character. It is a refreshingly democratic and supportive reimagination of a building: anti-ego, and almost anti-architecture.

Lacaton & Vassal demonstrates a wider view of architecture, of it having a greater imperative than itself. I share this view, along with an interest in democratic spaces and the potential of socially responsive architecture to empower, enable and enrich.

Lacaton & Vassal also, I now realise, employs a similar design approach – one of continuous critical dialogue, both within the office and with stakeholders, beneficiaries and more than 100 collaborators. Not surprisingly, with such strong artist and community ties, Palais de Tokyo is deeply rooted, and the space is meaningful to lots of people.

There is a similarity of ambition to Cedric Price's Fun Palace in that it was completely flexible and permeable, to encourage visitors to come in and engage with the artists and the art. Perhaps the nearest equivalent we have in the UK to this in spirit is the Royal Festival Hall foyer.

Lacaton & Vassal's inspiration was the Jemaa el-Fnaa square in the heart of Marrakesh, and they wanted the Palais to similarly enable all manner of uses.

There are some obvious parallels with our TNG Youth & Community Centre for Lewisham council, which is primarily about providing a positive, vibrant and inclusive space that users can take ownership of. To achieve this result, you have to provide a backdrop that's neither too prescriptive nor rich. It's not minimal architecture, but is instead an architecture of necessity – simple, efficient and entirely legible.

When some of the marble column linings were found to be loose, Lacaton & Vassal neither removed nor reinstalled to match the existing, choosing instead a simple metal strap to keep them on. It couldn't really be any cheaper and yet there's something very beautiful and rich about it.

This building strikes even more of a chord now. Having set up RCKa, I appreciate how difficult it is to retain the clarity of an idea and realise a building's social purpose, seemingly against all odds, as Lacaton & Vassal did here.

Tim Riley

At Palais de Tokyo, Lacaton & Vassal went beyond the role of the architect, becoming instead more like a custodian of the building with a comprehensive and strategic understanding of the client's needs.

Flexibility and adaptability were identified as the main drivers. Lacaton & Vassal didn't dictate what type of art could be shown where by over-designing for a particular type of work, but instead had the humility and vision to provide an infrastructure for things to happen anywhere. What's important in this project is not so much what the architects did, but more what they chose not to do.

There were stringent rules about not taking elements out. And Lacaton & Vassal's interventions are as transparent as possible to maintain visual routes through the building. Circulation is not dictated. Instead, people are trusted to decide how to explore it for themselves, flowing where they want in order to enjoy the rooms they find most attractive. It is principally a series of flexible spaces for things to happen in, primed for improvisation and imbued with potential.

Inside, there is no attempt to attenuate the space in terms of sound. Normally, the acoustics would be controlled to reduce reverberation but Palais de Tokyo just celebrates the audio, which adds a certain kind of informality as it all just blurs together. It's all part of the democratic nature of the gallery – here you can do anything and as a result you're not intimidated because of the acoustics.

Its democratic spirit is evidenced by the eschewing of the original grand entrance. Instead, a conscious decision was made to utilise a less intimidating front entrance on an upper level. You can witness how positively this is felt by visitors as they experience the surprise of entering into a vast playground behind the imposing fresco of the host building.

Russell Curtis

It was only when RCKa went through the Young Architect of the Year Award interview process in 2011 that we really started to distil our approach to the design of public buildings, and the similarities between this and Lacaton & Vassal's work started to become apparent.

Lacaton & Vassal invested a lot in this project, relocating its office to it during the first phase.

Living with the building day-to-day provided the practice with the perfect opportunity to fully understand and respond inventively to the existing fabric. Nothing is arbitrary, everything is purposeful and there is no embellishment. It is a bottom-up, responsive solution rather than the application of a predetermined dogma.

Lacaton & Vassal was, however, rigorous about presenting no artifice, preferring to retain and add to the many layers of occupation it found. What's nice is that it's not precious. You're not scared about touching it because it's already so bashed around. It's so different to the pristine white cube galleries of its neighbour, the Museum of Modern Art.

While it had a greater budget for phase two works, Lacaton & Vassal stuck to the same approach. It is grand in scale, but feels welcoming. The architects talk about learning from agricultural buildings and this certainly informs details such as the rooflights in the top gallery.

For a gallery building, the servicing strategy was pared back. There is no air-conditioning because Lacaton & Vassal understood that it would have required huge ducts, which would have been expensive and visually problematic, and so it carried out extensive modelling to show that it wasn't needed.

It found the exposed concrete structure particularly attractive and worked to keep it in its found state. By stripping away the superficiality of the original design, with its thin marble veneer, the architects make us reflect on what is really important about the building: space, light and use.

Entrance of the Palais de Tokyo, a gallery building originally built for the 1937 International Exhibition of Arts and Technology.

ROUGH AND READY Although the Palais de Tokyo itself was established in 2002, it occupies an Art Deco building constructed in 1937 as the Palais des Musées d'Art Moderne. This formed part of the International Exhibition of Arts and Technology, located near the Eiffel Tower.

It was used as an arts venue in several guises after the exhibition. An attempt to turn it into a cinema complex was abandoned in 1995 and the building was closed for several years before its government-instigated return to gallery use.

Bordeaux practice Lacaton & Vassal won a competition for a €3 million refurbishment of just 7,800sq m of the building. Dedicated to the emerging contemporary art scene, the gallery was conceived as a "found" space. Deliberately rough and ready, it was never regarded as finished, but instead as a space with potential to evolve. A second phase in 2012 by the same architects provided 16,500sq m more accommodation.

Inside the entrance foyer new interventions are clearly visible within the stripped-back fabric of the original exhibition building.

Individual Houses

Simon Hudspith on the
roof of Castle Drogo, which
abstracted classic features
of medieval castles.

Castle Drogo

Location: Drewsteignton, Devon, UK

Architect: Edwin Lutyens

Completed: 1911–30

Chosen by Simon Hudspith of Panter Hudspith Architects

Castle Drogo is an intriguing mix of metaphor and folly that its architect Edwin Lutyens balanced incredibly well.

Lutyens made his name with fantastic country houses. These had a certain robustness, within a given set of rules – but I think he produced his best work when he started abstracting more, as he did at Drogo. Here the issues he dealt with were so much more complex – this wasn't just a large house surrounded by garden walls deep in the home counties. Instead, it has a much broader influence in the landscape and is very prominent as you approach from the surrounding area. The symbolic issues it dealt with are much bigger too, as Lutyens tried to condense history for his client who had this great romantic idea of a castle.

In some ways, Drogo is a baronial castle that embodies the idea of landed gentry having a country seat, and it fits so perfectly the idea of an Englishman's home is his castle. It was the last castle to be built in England and was commissioned by Julius Drewe, a very successful grocer who retired when he was 33. With time on his hands, he was looking to establish a built ancestry. The family had a connection to the village of Drewsteignton in Devon – named after Drogo de Teigne who reputedly came over with William the Conqueror – and Drewe bought 180ha of land formerly owned by Drogo with the intention of building his own family heritage.

The idea that Drewe could buy that heritage with the help of Lutyens' designs proved an interesting starting point. Drewe had a romantic view of castles that Lutyens domesticated at Castle Drogo. There are many castle symbols within the building but they tend not to be literal and there is, to some extent, the idea

that here was someone trying to buy their own history by building a folly. At the time there were far more contemporary architectural ideas developing in Europe and so Drogo was in a sense going against the modern movement.

What's intriguing, however, is how Lutyens avoids making Drogo a folly through his clever use and interpretation of the symbols traditionally associated with 'castleness'. The house is most castle-like at the entrance, with the heraldic lion over the door, the working portcullis and the castellated tower – and generally there's a lot of Tudor in Drogo, especially the proportions of the windows.

As the project progressed, I think Lutyens became less interested in the folly aspect and more interested in interpretations of 'castleness'.

He started abstracting details – playing down the whole issue of castellation by making the crenellations flatter and the whole composition a lot plainer.

Lutyens changed classic medieval castle features such as the arrow slots so that they read as contemporary slots in the masonry instead. The notion of carving is very strong. Walls start as a large block of stone at their base then become more refined and articulated as they elevate, becoming more sculptural at the ends. Every now and then he carves into these blocks to signify an entrance, a niche or a support for a bay window.

Inside, Lutyens had the difficulty of responding to a client who was repeatedly changing his mind. But despite the building being a third of its intended size, he still managed to produce a sequence of very beautiful rooms. His skill

is in the distortion of scale, often choosing quite traditional features, such a stone arches, cornices and bay windows, but then changing their scale to produce a more delicate and intimate atmosphere.

The grand staircase down to the dining room, lined with granite and projecting bay windows, has all the hallmarks of a castle, but once you are inside feels quite domestic and extremely well judged. Even in the kitchen he could not resist yet more ambiguity – creating a 'chapel for food' with domed ceiling and lantern that illuminates the circular 'prep' table flanked by a choir of wooden plate racks.

I've visited Drogo four times over 25 years. I found it particularly helpful in 2002 when Panter Hudspith was embarking on early design work for the Museum of Lincoln. We'd just spent five years working in York, another medieval city, and I was very interested in the challenge of how to position contemporary buildings into historic settings. We spent a lot of time looking at medieval cities and I really appreciated how in these you could find a whole range of buildings which had an understanding and respect for each other even though there weren't any planners policing them.

The Museum of Lincoln is halfway up the hill in Lincoln which forms a link between the historic area at the top and the industrialised area at the bottom. I was looking for buildings that tried to embody and deal with a whole set of historical issues and found the idea of abstracting and reinterpreting historic iconography that Lutyens explored at Drogo very useful as a reference. Another inspiration for us was Drogo's materiality, in particular its refinement and crafting of stone.

Castle Drogo works as an experience. It is a great place to go and visit and I think it would have been a great place to live. But one of its most intriguing aspects is that even though it wasn't finished, unlike medieval towns, it has had no incremental development. The whole process of castle building means that they are never completely finished, but evolve over hundreds of years with different people adding different parts over time. Drogo took 20 years to construct, which is a long time to build a contemporary building but is nothing for a castle. Today our culture has frozen its heritage by listing buildings and not letting them evolve as they would have done in the past.

Castle Drogo was really the last gasp for these types of buildings. By the time it was finished in the 1930s, our culture had moved on forever.

South elevation of the castle. Lutyens' original design included a great hall to the south, which was never built.

BUILDING HERITAGE Drogo was famously the last castle to be built in England, and was designed by Edwin Lutyens for Julius Drewe, founder of the Home & Colonial Stores. The Grade I listed castle, set above the Teign Gorge, took 20 years to build and was originally intended to be much larger.

Despite its external historic references, the castle internally reflected Drewe's interest in innovation, with electricity and lifts incorporated from the start. Plans for a great hall were abandoned and the base was turned into a chapel and gun room. Lutyens also designed the garden, with planting by Gertrude Jekyll.

Drewe died just one year after the castle's completion. Drogo was given to the National Trust in 1974 – the first twentieth-century property it took on. The Trust is currently overseeing a £11 million restoration to deal with persistent water ingress.

Castle Drogo's imposing castellated main entrance features a working portcullis and a heraldic relief of a lion.

Above left: The granite-vaulted main staircase leading down to the dining room.

Above right: Kitchen, conceived as a "chapel for food" with domed ceiling lantern above a circular 'prep' table.

Right: Entrance hall. Like most of the interior, this is quite domestic in character and contrasts with the castle's imposing exterior.

Above: E-1027, recently restored, overlooking the French Riviera. John Tuomey first visited the house when it was a "lyrically very beautiful" ruin.

Opposite: Mural by houseguest Le Corbusier added ten years after the villa was completed.

E-1027

Location: Roquebrune-Cap-Martin, France
Architect: Eileen Gray
Completed: 1926–29
Chosen by John Tuomey of O'Donnell + Tuomey

When Sheila [O'Donnell] and I were students in Dublin in the 1970s there was an Eileen Gray exhibition at the Bank of Ireland just as she was being re-discovered.

We both got this strong sense of a pioneering, extraordinary, pre-feminist architect/designer and became fascinated by her work, which is very subtle and sensitive. She was an extraordinary woman who had so many talents and followed her curiosity from Japanese lacquer work to furniture to architecture. She was very retiring and practically disappeared herself, which made her all the more intriguing. We also became quite fanatical about Le Corbusier and one of the things that brought me and Sheila together was travelling to see purist early modern houses in Paris and trying to track down traces of Eileen Gray's work.

Then at some point, about 15 years or so ago, Sheila and I made a little pilgrimage down to Cap-Martin to see E-1027 and Corbusier's Le Cabanon. We walked around the house and tried to get in but were put off by the fierce guard dog. Overgrown and dishevelled, it was in a state of ruin, which made it lyrically very beautiful. It looked like a shipwreck but a very beautiful, sure-footed one.

It's a strangely isolated site. You don't appreciate before you go there just how close E-1027 is to Le Cabanon. Corbusier built it 30 years later but had spotted the adjacent site when he visited Eileen. Whereas Eileen Gray had an extremely luxurious sensibility to space and fabric, Corbusier had a mad Spartan strain to him, as is clear at Le Cabanon.

Both Sheila and I have studied E-1027 quite a bit and we particularly appreciate her special sensitivity in making sequential or polycentric spaces. There's a beautiful plan of the house by Gray where she drew lines of a person's movement across the surface of the plan to show how they might move around the space as they go to, for example, the wardrobe, then turn on their heel, and go the window, then turn on their heel and so on. Her lines trace the ritual of routine habitation, and it is very interesting to consider how space is experienced sequentially as well as in a linear way. This is something Gray has a particular sensitivity for.

I do have some misgivings about the idea of going back to see the house again now that it has been restored – sometimes the poetic memory of a ruin and its feeling of potential can be more vibrant than the rescued reality. But one day we'd like to go and actually make it though the door this time rather than see it from the outside. A journey to that location brings you not just to E-1027 and Corbusier's Cabanon but also to the nearby (since relocated to Sligo) grave of WB Yeats, who was buried there as war broke out. What more could a travelling Irish architect want?

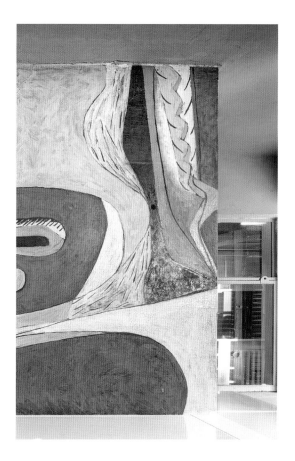

VISIONARY VILLA E-1027 was designed in 1926-29 as a summer house by Irish designer Eileen Gray (1878–1976) with her partner Jean Badovici. It takes its name from the position of their initials in the alphabet – E for Eileen, 10 for J, 2 for B and 7 for Gray.

The modernist villa was built over two storeys into a terrace on a hillside overlooking the French Riviera, and featured built-in and separate furniture designed by Gray including her famous E-1027 side table. Le Corbusier, who was later to build his Cabanon retreat on an adjacent site, visited the house in 1938-89 as a guest of Badovici and added his own murals. The house fell into neglect for many years before being taken into public ownership and restored as part of the Cap Moderne site.

Jonathan Woolf outside
the back of Haus Lange,
one of a pair of brick villas
at Krefeld that helped
inform his own work.

Haus Esters and Haus Lange

Location: Krefeld, Germany

Architect: Ludwig Mies van der Rohe

Completed: 1927–30

Chosen by Jonathan Woolf of Jonathan Woolf Architects

In 1998 I was commissioned to design a house on the edge of Hampstead Heath that later became known as Brick Leaf House. The client had originally wanted a modernist white pavilion but our approach was that, given its position, we should use brick. I'd never built in brick, so began researching brick buildings and travelled to Krefeld to see these two neighbouring Mies houses.

When I visited, they were in the middle of being restored and the structure was exposed. To me, peering through the wire fence, this was incredibly revealing – they were built like battleships, with something like 50,000kg of meticulously bolted steel beams and columns to hold up all that brick as well as the floors. These are complex hybrids and that set me off using a similar construction at Brick Leaf House.

What's revealing is how Mies tried to hide these houses from his oeuvre. He wanted to be understood as the new classicist and what didn't conform to that story was edited out. When I studied Mies as a student, the Krefeld houses weren't even mentioned. It wasn't until 1995 that Kenneth Frampton's essay 'Mies van der Rohe: Avant-Garde and Continuity' put them back into the story of his work.

I was also interested that they were a pair. I wanted to explore the connection between the two, as Brick Leaf house was originally going to be two houses for two brothers. Visiting Haus Lange and Haus Esters was a way of testing the plausibility of designing two buildings side by side in a formal relationship.

The plans are certainly neither classical nor pure. Each house is marginally different from the other. In the published plans, rooms are labelled 'Man's Room, Woman's Room, Child's Room', a degree of functionalisation which I have never come across before or since. But the key move of making the main living room face north to the street rather than south to the garden is curious.

It's clear though that this main room was conceived as a kind of shop front for formal entertainment, as opposed to the day-to-day rooms that orientate to the garden. It looks as though the client wanted the ability to keep the two realms separate.

As for the first floors, although each holds the same accommodation, Lange has en suite internal bathrooms that demand an awkward lowered corridor ceiling and front façade while Esters opts for a central corridor and bathroom outside the room, so the façade parapet remains constant. Five of the six Esters bedrooms are linked together enfilade, but none of Lange's are. Almost no walls in either house align vertically: spatial composition is the *a priori* language and structural implications are consciously transgressed. In the gradual undressing of Mies's constructional logic over the decades, this project offers the most potent graffiti within his oeuvre.

Perhaps Mies would've preferred to have one building since the contradictions are made more visible through their pairing. On the other hand, Lange was an extremely powerful industrialist who was instrumental in Mies getting his next 10 commissions – clearly not someone to fall out with.

Mies's discontent seems to have been a general malaise rather than just frustration at not using more glass. Haus Esters and Haus Lange were for real clients with real problems and the result was more of a compromise.

Yet you can certainly imagine enjoying them as homes. There is a generosity of openness with different rooms to dwell in. On the garden side, the houses step back to give a serrated edge to follow the sun's path. Mies was said to be frustrated at the window size but when you visit, they seem enormous. The houses have a substantial solidity to them (walls are 60cm deep) despite these large window openings which lighten it up and frame views in a powerful way.

They were always places to display art and that accounts for the large amount of wall space that Mies was asked to provide. He shows that you can have generous windows and still have generous walls. In this way, the houses can achieve an intimacy his others couldn't, and I love buildings where you can't determine what's going on inside.

One-off houses seem at first to be a great opportunity to showcase your architecture but they are possibly the ultimate challenge because they are inhabited in a very particular way. An acid test is whether such buildings can take on other activities beyond their roles as family houses. A good building should be able to outlast its initial functional purpose and be inhabited in many different ways.

I am intrigued by the way artists have used the Krefeld buildings as something to respond to and re-interpret rather than simply hang their work in. It is precisely because of the ambiguities present in the architecture that it has borne such fruit.

From visiting Krefeld, I learnt that there was nothing particular to be gained from two such close designs so close together. Meanwhile, the more my Brick Leaf House clients discussed

what they wanted, the more it made sense to have their two houses as a single form. I was already thinking of using steel but wanted to see the Mies buildings at Krefeld in the flesh to understand how it worked, and this confirmed that was the best structural approach to take. There are extremely large spans that would be more difficult to create in anything other than steel.

It's clear that Mies won some battles with his clients and lost others. Studying them anew, it feels as though the Krefeld houses Haus Lange and Haus Esters, taken together, are an anagram of the ideal.

HYBRID PAIR Hermann Lange, a wealthy textile manufacturer and art collector, commissioned Mies van der Rohe to design a private house for him in 1927. This led to a commission to design a house for his friend Herr Esters on the adjacent site.

The two villas were completed to different but complementary designs and were intended as 'museum houses' to display their owners' private collections. Mies did not regard the houses as successful and did not like to discuss them. They were only widely recognised as a major part of his oeuvre when they were included in an exhibition on Mies at New York's MoMA 10 years ago.

Art exhibitions have been staged in Haus Lange since 1955 and Haus Esters since 1981, when the house became part of the Krefeld Kunstmuseen. Both houses underwent extensive restoration at the end of the last century.

Left: The garden rooms step back to give a serrated edge to the rear of the house.

Opposite: Haus Lange with Haus Esters to the left. The houses were designed as a pair but are similar rather than identical.

Maison de Verre, admired
by Richard Rogers for
its 'inventiveness and
technological wonder'
as well as its translucent
screen of glass bricks.

Maison de Verre

Location: Paris, France
Architect: Pierre Chareau, Bernard Bijvoet
Completed: 1927–32
Chosen by Richard Rogers of Rogers Stirk Harbour + Partners

Peter Smithson, my tutor in my final year at the Architectural Association told me about Maison de Verre. In 1959, I visited this beautiful house in Paris together with my girlfriend (later my first wife) Su, and was entranced by it – it became the subject of my first published article, a feature in *Domus*. The house remains an inspiration to me.

Some 15 years later, Ruthie and I were living in Paris, and Ruthie was pregnant with our son Roo. Her doctor Dr Vellay was the son-in-law of Jean Dalsace, who had commissioned the Maison de Verre. Like his father-in-law, he had his surgery there, so revisiting Maison de Verre for consultations gave me the opportunity to become reacquainted with this amazing building.

Maison de Verre is quite unlike any normal house where windows would be placed on each floor. Instead, the house's structure of glass bricks creates a single unbroken elevation, very much like a Japanese screen. It's crystal, but like cut crystal you can't actually see through it. Instead it is translucent, neither opaque nor transparent. This very Eastern concept and how it plays with concepts of transparency is one of the most exciting things about the house.

This translucent screen contrasts with the solidity of one of the few fixed elements – a single column that holds up the top-floor flat that the existing tenant refused to leave when it was built. The column is near the entrance, painted red and black with these great bolts showing. You can understand it, enjoy it, stroke it – it is a real piece of artisanship, and an example of the creativity that can be unlocked by constraint.

One of the high points is stepping onto the main staircase, which in my opinion is possibly the greatest staircase of this century. The fine wires that hold the door open, the new type of hinge, are all inventiveness and technological wonder. Then as you walk forwards it's like stepping onto a magic carpet that's about to fly away as it leads you into the salon of Maison de Verre.

From the salon, you can see the translucence of the wall of light in full. The light is refracted through the glass to give an even brightness, a soft, glowing light. Then we see the series of columns that support the flat above and the ingenious window.

Visiting the Maison de Verre is like being inside a beautiful lantern – everything shines, everything moves, everything is changeable. It is a modernist expression of technology that was unequalled through the 1930s, and for some time after. All the windows can be opened simultaneously quite easily by turning a handle. Another machine, a little mobile staircase, is made with an amazing economy of means to do the maximum amount of work with the least amount of material.

The client, Dr Dalsace, must have been amazingly understanding – he was way out on a limb. I can't think of a client who would accept a blank screen of glass bricks on the outside wall, and I've had some terrific clients.

But he had an amazingly brilliant design team to propose it. Together, they achieved this moment of enlightenment that I feel can only be compared with the highest peaks of Western culture. I really do feel that Maison de Verre is that important.

GLASS LANTERN Maison de Verre (House of Glass) was built for Dr Jean and Annie Dalsace to house a home and gynaecologist's office. An alteration of an eighteenth-century building, the design had to create new accommodation beneath a retained top floor flat (whose occupant refused to move). The solution was the use of a projected steel-framed rear façade entirely of glass blocks above a recessed ground floor foyer. Inside, this double-height space is occupied by the main living room.

Created by architect Bernard Bijvoet with furniture designer Pierre Chareau and metal craftsman Louis Dalbet, the interior is characterised by the great detail of its fittings including movable partitions and retractable upper stairs from the sitting room to Mme Dalsace's bedroom.

The house was a popular salon for Paris intellectuals in the 1930s before the owners had to flee the Nazis. It was bought from the Dalsace family in 2005 by American collector Robert Rubin and subsequently restored.

David Kohn in the garden room of Villa Necchi. Here, plants grow between panes of glass: "it's like the garden is stored in the walls".

Villa Necchi Campiglio

Location: Milan, Italy
Architect: Piero Portaluppi
Completed: 1932–35
Chosen by David Kohn of David Kohn Architects

If you know of Piero Portaluppi's work you are likely to have a connection to Milan as there's nothing published on the architect in English. I was introduced to his work at Vila Necchi by a Milanese friend and architect, Massimo Curzi, a few years ago. I remember it felt like an ancient house in a modern idiom. I've been back four times since; there's a kind of magic there and I find it very inspiring.

Portaluppi is not a pivotal historical architect like his near contemporary Giò Ponti – Portaluppi's work is comparatively a much more difficult prospect. Villa Necchi is quite testing as a building in parts, but I think it has something very special about it.

There's a tension in the house between architectures of the nineteenth and the twentieth centuries. Is it a proto-modernist villa or is it a nineteenth-century villa brought into the twentieth century? Is it art deco?

The term eclectic is sometimes used pejoratively but I really appreciate the things that hover between. It represents the promise of and the antidote to the modern project – sufficiently modern to not be a stifling nineteenth-century pastiche, but not throwing the baby out with the bathwater and becoming a mechanistic intellectual exercise in newness and eradicating distinctions.

Villa Necchi is in a very well-to-do part of Milan. It was commissioned by a wealthy family who made their money from sewing machines. I appreciate patronage where the client and architect clearly went into great detail about every aspect of the house. It's rare.

Formally, the house is simple, with no gymnastics. Rather, the architecture is

fascinating for how it sets up nuanced relationships between different uses, between different times of day, and between inside and outside. Everything is choreographed to have a legible hierarchy. There's a pleasure imagined in every corner that is palpable. It would be lovely to live there, for a while.

Inside, there's a grand enfilade of rooms but within these are separate datums and the spaces of the rooms are often much larger than the social settings themselves which sit happily within them. The lessons for public and semi-public spaces at a different scale are evident. There's both intimacy and space for conviviality. It's just waiting for people to come in and have a great evening.

The entrances are significant because being enfilade rooms, there are no corridors and you have to pass through every room to get to the next. All the doorways have sliding screens that disappear into the wall so that it can be read either as one space or as separate rooms.

The garden room is one of my favourite rooms in the world. It is like a dream space. There are these very big expanses of window on two sides with a sliver of ferns between two planes of glass. It's like the garden is stored in the walls. If you sit down on the sofas, you can't see the ground outside so it feels like you're up in the trees. There's also a delicious Portaluppi-designed lapis lazuli table and a marble floor that appears woven like tartan. But it all reads as a delightful whole.

In the library, the ceiling is quite brilliant. It is an asymmetrical diamond pattern with a theme of weaving that you can also see in the marble floors. It creates a sense of tension across the room. This is integral to one's perception of the

form and weight and structure overhead, which seems as light as fabric, as though stretched. Portaluppi designed amazing details and the level of craftsmanship right down to the hinges is extraordinary. Although it's very well made, it does not feel gluttonous. Here, it feels like a background setting to heighten the comfort and pleasure of those using it.

There's the incredible, veneered staircase opposite the entrance; the mirrored, diamond-patterned screens to the dining room; the goat leather panelling on the dining room walls, and the personalised Portaluppi-designed crockery, for example.

The dining room is a place where the mix of architects involved – Portaluppi and Tomaso Buzzi, who worked on the house after the Second World War – is really problematic and it lapses into kitsch.

Upstairs, I love the star window – from the outside you wonder which room it's in and then you go upstairs and find he's put it in the toilet. It's very playful.

In the work we do, I often try to find extremes – something very open yet very intimate and comfortable. A trick is to create smaller spaces through openings and niches like at Villa Necchi, where the architecture invites movement and change.

Portaluppi was influenced by different things at different periods in his life. I try to look at different architectures in history and how these can be assimilated into a new language. Villa Necchi has also taught me how the divisions between rooms are important, and how the architecture is inflected to invite certain kinds of uses, whether it's a huge window overlooking

the garden, or the lobby to a dining room where you gather before the doors are opened. Despite the materials and the geometries, Villa Necchi forms a background, a setting for its inhabitants' use. It's clearly not saying that a background has to be neutral and bland. Instead it is rich and retains a kind of informality that allows you to choose to occupy it rather than feel that you're being put on show.

There are a few things my practice has referenced directly from Portaluppi's work. Our interior for the Carrer Avinyó apartment in Barcelona followed a Portaluppi pattern but in different colours and framed glass spaces that are like internal winter gardens. Our house in Norfolk for Stuart Shave has a sequence of rooms partly informed by the Villa Necchi.

The Villa Necchi is not perfect, or rather it is not trying to be perfect. Instead, there are tensions in the architecture that make it challenging and invigorating. That was perhaps a source of pleasure for Portaluppi when designing the house. And so it is for me.

Above: View towards the garden room with the house entrance to the far right. Villa Necchi sits in generous grounds in the heart of Milan.

Opposite, left: An asymmetric ceiling pattern in the ceiling of the library carries on the theme of weaving also found in marble floors elsewhere in the house.

Opposite, right: Entrance hall and staircase with veneered walls, one of the many hand-crafted details found throughout the house.

HIGH SOCIETY Villa Necchi Campiglio was built for a wealthy Lombard industrialist family – Angelo Campiglio, his wife Gigina Necchi and her sister Nedda Necchi – between 1932–5.

They commissioned Piero Portaluppi, a fashionable society architect, to design a home that was modern but at the same time luxurious, comfortable and suitable for their sociable, entertaining lifestyle. Tomaso Buzzi updated the house in the 1950s, replacing some of Portaluppi's modern designs with his more traditional look, preferring antiques, draperies and elaborate chandeliers.

When Gigina Necchi died in 2001 at the age of 99, she bequeathed the house to the FAI (the Italian equivalent of the National Trust) and it was restored, and then reopened for visitors. It now houses a collection of mid-twentieth-century Italian art that was not part of the original interior. It was also the location for the Tilda Swinton film *I Am Love*.

Chris Williamson revisits the "incredibly inspiring" Eames House, designed by Charles and Ray Eames as part of the Case Study House Program.

Eames House (Case Study House #8)

Location: Pacific Palisades, Los Angeles, California
Design: Charles and Ray Eames (adapting a scheme designed with Eero Saarinen)
Completed: 1945–49
Chosen by Chris Williamson of Weston Williamson

The Eames House has got everything I love about architecture – rigour and thoroughness but also playfulness and colour, with everything beautifully detailed. As one of the Case Study Houses instigated by *Arts and Architecture* magazine in the mid-1940s, it typified an era of invention and excellence in modern domestic architecture. It's an incredibly inspiring building.

I first went to see it in 1980 after working in New York for Welton Becket and before returning to London to work for Michael Hopkins. I had visited other Case Study Houses and those of Frank Lloyd Wright but the elegance and simplicity of the Eames House was stunning, and one of the many highlights of my time in America.

I already knew quite a bit about the house before visiting because I'd read Andrew Weston's diploma dissertation on it. But it was still fantastic to see it in reality. Ray was still living there and anyone could just turn up, wander around outside and go into the downstairs workshop.

It's a demonstration house, as much as anything else, to show just how much you can do with industrial system building – you can design a very rational building constructed using industrial materials but still create something interesting with Mondrian colours and double-height spaces. The spatial variety within the Eames House is an inspiration.

The other thing I love about the house is the way it relates to the landscape. The tall eucalyptus trees are as elegantly beautiful as the house itself and the two complement each other. The amazing thing is that the original plans show that this was not the initial intention – it was only during the time that

the pre-fabricated industrial components were ordered from the catalogue and were delivered that Charles and Ray fell in love with the meadow and decided to reconfigure and build the modular steel house further back to preserve it and better integrate the house into the landscape.

According to the Eames Foundation, the house was envisaged as serving as a background for what Charles called "life in work" with the surrounding nature as a "shock absorber".

I'd love to build something like this but it's virtually impossible to find a similar site in London where you could do something that modern. What's really nice about the Eames House is its lightness of structure, which would be very difficult to achieve using modern levels of insulation. Instead of using single-glazing and SIP insulated panels like Eames did, you'd have to have a completely different design philosophy and the house would turn out quite differently.

But I'm sure that if the Eameses and those other Case Study architects were around today they'd be doing something really innovative with sustainability.

When I returned to London after my time in America it was fantastic to work in Michael and Patty Hopkins' home/office, which was a contextual interpretation along similar industrial lines to the Eames House using Metsec beams and built in a similar sort of leafy setting. Both houses are stunning and have been an inspiration for our 30 years at Weston Williamson.

I have been back three times since, and it's stood the test of time really well. It's the sort

of place that's just good to come back to again and again. To me it represents a particular time of hope and optimism in the future. New materials, new ways of thinking and living and new ideas. It inspired a generation.

CASE STUDY The Eames House was the eighth in the Case Study House Program instigated by *Arts and Architecture* magazine in the mid-1940s. This challenged architects to create a series of modern homes for real or hypothetical clients using materials and techniques derived from those used in the Second World War.

The first scheme was designed by Charles Eames and Eero Saarinen in 1945 using pre-fabricated materials. When the steel arrived on site in 1948, Charles and Ray Eames reconfigured the design using the same materials and repositioned the modular steel house on the site to better integrate the house into the landscape. Only one extra beam was needed. The house was completed in 1949. Charles and Ray Eames lived there until their deaths in 1978 and 1988 respectively.

Marie-José van Hee on the stepped terrace at Maison Louis Carré, which she admires as a "total work" of architecture and design.

Maison Louis Carré

Loaction: Bazoches-sur-Guyonne, France
Architect: Alvar Aalto
Completed: 1956–59
Chosen by Marie-José van Hee

During my studies I was enthusiastic about Scandinavian architecture, which had a completely different character to what we knew in Belgium. I had visited Denmark to see housing by Arne Jacobsen but I hadn't gone any further north so I only knew Alvar Aalto's architecture through plans and photos in books, in particular a book on Aalto that a friend gave to me in 1979. This was the first way I got to know Maison Louis Carré.

I was astonished when I saw his sketches, which were rough, intuitive and not at all academic. I liked to sketch in the same way but at university we were taught to design more academically and in these days – before computers – I wasn't very good at doing correct 3D design. Aalto's sketches showed me that it was OK to be intuitive in how you design, and this encouraged me to carry on.

Although I'd studied the plans and the sections, it was only when I visited Maison Louis Carré that the house really came alive for me. This is a house you feel free in. Aalto made houses for others which he felt he could live in himself – and Maison Louis Carré feels as if it was designed for people who were really happy to make a house to sit so well in that beautiful landscape. It is a very good house in terms of scale and intimacy. The proportions and choice of materials make you feel completely at home because of the very human scale of the rooms, and the relationship to each other and the landscape. The dimensions are just right.

I particularly like how you enter the house. This journey starts with the way Aalto organised the approach from the gate. Visitors can just see the house up ahead through the trees from the entrance and this makes you curious. But you still have a way to go to get there and the road curves around before coming up to the porch and its canopy. Rather than being added onto the façade, this canopy feels as if it was cut out of the volume of the house, and so it seems like you're already inside the house before you even enter. You are protected, and the canopy is a way of inviting you in.

Once inside, the entrance hall is about much more than just receiving people. Louis Carré had a great collection of art and photographs and these were originally displayed on two walls that made a kind of mini gallery in the reception and divided the public space from the privacy of the bedrooms. The paintings are detached from the walls and hang in the space itself. Just as the house sits well in the contours of the landscape, you have the feeling that the paintings belonged in the home too.

Aalto understood how to create a good atmosphere. You turn right to go down half a level to the living room and – wow! – there's this wonderful diagonal view through the huge window over the garden as it slopes away down the hill. The curve of the ceiling with its wooden slats gives a real sense of movement as it sweeps down beautifully.

I enjoy that you can see that the living room carries on around the corner, but you don't know how far it carries on until you get there. And I like how the fireplace juts out slightly at the corner so that when you walk around into the room, you're not just walking around a wall but around another element. Aalto's living rooms always have a chimney and open fire for people to sit together. This sense of community is something I like to create in my own work. Aalto has provided it here, although for the French it is perhaps not as important as it is for Nordic people with their colder, darker climate.

Maison Louis Carré is a total work from the landscape, to the house, to the design of the furniture and the lamps. Everything, even the furniture in the servant's rooms upstairs, is beautifully designed. It is a house full of details, but whereas art nouveau houses can sometimes feel overpowering, you never have that feeling inside Maison Louis Carré.

Even in the kitchen, the beautiful wooden trim under the marble worktop is designed so that when you sit against it, your legs don't touch the cold surface. Such details are very important and they are everywhere, such as the way Aalto keeps the entrance to the bedrooms set back and concealed by a curtain to preserve the intimacy of the couple's private space.

Lamps were very important to Aalto. People living in the north of Europe have to be careful of how they treat light because there are only a few hours of daylight in winter. Aalto designed a particularly special one in the dining room at Maison Louis Carré that shines light in two directions – both on the art on the walls and down. And on the way up to the house, Aalto designed lamp-posts that are like flowers, with a big shell-like petal for a reflector. Every time I see them they give me a shiver of pleasure.

I like the way Aalto uses the slope of the landscape in the design of this house, creating terracing to make a very successful relationship between the house and the swimming pool down the hill.

I don't yet know all the ways in which my work will be influenced by Maison Louis Carré. This house overcomes you and goes right into your inner map, your personal library, and you never know when and how it will come out again, until it does.

Above: View towards the living room. Maison Louis Carré "overcomes you and goes right into your inner map" says Marie –José van Hee.

Opposite: The swimming pool and pool house, with the main house at the top of the site to the left.

AALTO GEM Designed for a French art dealer and collector, Maison Louis Carré is Alvar Aalto's only remaining building in France and a total work of architecture, interior and landscape design.

The villa is clad in local stone from Chartres, lime-washed bricks, copper and wood, and has a blue slate roof. The entire interior including fittings, furniture and textiles, was designed by Aalto or his collaborators. The ground floor is arranged on two levels around a large entrance hall with a red pine ceiling, and is divided into a public zone (hall, cloakroom, living room, library, dining room), the private zone (three bedrooms, three bathrooms, sauna) and the service zone of kitchen, pantry, larder, staff dining room. The main bedrooms have private terraces that lead to terraced steps descending to the pool. Staff bedrooms are on the first floor.

Aalto also designed the 3 ha garden, entrance gate and garage, and in 1963 added a swimming pool and pool house.

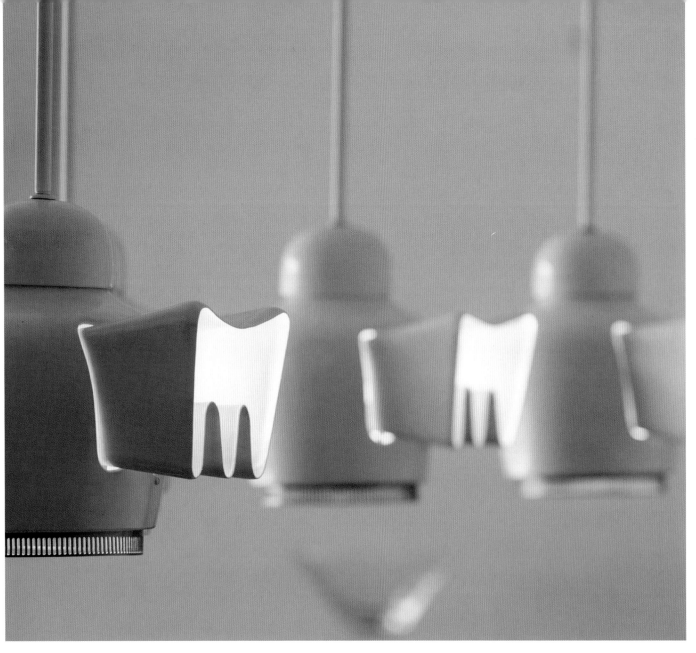

Above: Detail of lights in the dining room. Lights were particularly important to Aalto, and he designed many for Maison Louis Carré.

Right: Living room, with fireplace to the left and views over the landscape through generous windows to the right.

Hexenhaus

Location: Bad Karlshafen, Germany
Architects: Alison and Peter Smithson
Completed: 1986–2002
Chosen by Takero Shimazaki of Takero Shimazaki Architects

Takero Shimazaki at the Hexenhaus, a once modest cottage extended and altered over many years by architects Alison and Peter Smithson.

Being Japanese, a refined approach to design came naturally to me. But I find it difficult to just keep turning to beautiful and restrained work as an approach to design. The Smithsons gave me another way of approaching my own architecture. I'm not a big expert on them. I didn't research them as a student. Instead, my introduction to their work was more direct, meeting them as a family and then going to Germany to visit Axel Bruchhäuser's Hexenhaus home and their work at his Tecta furniture factory.

Axel and the Smithsons were a collaboration made in heaven. When they met, Axel said it was life-changing for them all. There is such sympathy at the heart of the architect-client relationship on the Hexenhaus. It's a gift. You can't learn it.

I got to know their work not by reading about it but through experience – my then practice partner Yuli Toh who knew Simon Smithson introduced them to me and asked if I'd like a few months off to work with Peter when he was working with Lorenzo Wong. It was very nice after co-running a practice and working mainly on a computer to go to an office where you'd spend the whole week drawing axonometrics with a pencil, and every detail and specification was written by hand. Details were celebrated. Everything was turned into a joy. Even something like having tea was a big ritual. I was given the task of drawing the bridge and lantern at Hexenhaus, which I found very challenging.

Everything was so carefully worked out, right down to the angle of a balustrade, for the sake of the joy of life. There was an appreciation of how the perception of different details could change your relationship to the outside world. Lorenzo and I would discuss this and ask Peter

why a detail was like it was – sometimes there was no answer. It just was. I thought it was so wonderful. It made me realise that time spent well is really crucial. You don't need hundreds of projects but you just need to do a few things really well.

I was only at Peter Smithson's studio for two months but I got so much from it, in particular this awareness of there being no boundaries between life, landscape, architecture and art. To the Smithsons, everything was an artfully constructed backdrop for activities for a richer life. Later, the Toh Shimazaki office came out to visit Hexenhaus in 2007 and this again completely changed how I look at architecture. Axel was there and he talked about how the Smithsons had tried to help his soul so that he could improve the lives of many through his company Tecta. It's not that precious as a building but it is precious about life. If you can find just one client-architect relationship like the one the Smithsons had with Axel in your career, that would be amazing. Developing the projects through the narrative of their respective cats was quite therapeutic for them – they saw the cats as themselves, but adding another voice to the discussions.

Photographs of the Hexenhaus might put off some architects who think it may look vernacular or folksy. But when you visit, you realise it's not about a style but about an approach to how spaces and places can be. The original house, with its Brothers Grimm roof and chimney in the wood, has been thoroughly decomposed through the various additions.

One of the things that interests me there is the application of the theory of 'conglomerate ordering' – the idea of additions over time. The order isn't obvious, or linear, but it is multi-

dimensional, based around the way Axel uses the house, specific views, and perceptions of the site over time. These perceptions seem quite intuitive and quite random at times. But there is a consistency of materiality and rhythm.

This house is one of the most successful in terms of looseness, which lots of architects struggle to create. I also appreciate how they accommodate maximum context and vernacular so that the architecture is the backdrop, even though there is a very strong sense of the architecture. But the Smithsons had the confidence to see the life of Axel and his cat Karlchen as much more important. There's a window seat for them to sit together, and a glass floor for Karlchen to look out for mice. Sometimes, the design is very specific, but sometimes it is without explanation, although there's definitely a system and an

ordering, based on experience, intuition and drawing things again and again. There's an incredible layering of views through the house and the forest. Is the landscape framing the architecture, or is the architecture framing the views?

After my time at their office, we [Toh Shimazaki Architecture] did OSh House in Surrey, which was so inspired by the Smithsons' way of working. We did collages, we stayed there before we got planning permission and mapped out on the site where the walls would be, really breathing in the site and absorbing Surrey English life – pubs, walking, the weather – just as the Smithsons absorbed the Hexenhaus context. Now we don't say no to really small projects if there is a potential for this quality. It's not about career, it's about enriching our environment.

When I visited Hexenhaus in 2007, I tended to view architecture more preciously, but now the boundaries are blurring between architecture and art and inhabitation. I've tried to convey some of these ideas to my own students at the AA: that architecture is a well-crafted and imaginative backdrop to what inhabitation can be. I am still pursuing these issues among other thoughts and I find it highly challenging.

Coming back again to Hexenhaus and seeing it in springtime, I can appreciate it afresh. It's a small jewel for me. It is truly a paradise on earth.

WOODLAND WONDER Hexenhaus (Witch House) was the site of a lengthy collaboration between Alison and Peter Smithson and Axel Bruchhäuser, owner of the Tecta furniture company. The Smithsons had already completed several projects at the nearby Tecta factory. The starting point for the Hexenhaus was a modest cottage in a wood, which the architects gradually evolved and extended through intense discussions with their client. Project communication was always by letter via a dialogue between the Smithsons' cat Snuff and Axel's cat Karlchen, who signed their letters with a paw stamp.

The Smithsons began with small interventions such as a new porch here, an opening there, gradually reworking and expanding the house. Their aim was always to create a harmonious environment of man, cat and trees through light, air, space and water. A tiny but beautifully appointed glass-floored retreat (Witch Broom Room) was built in 1997, reached from a high-level walkway off the bathroom. This was followed by the Tea Pavilion and Peter Smithson's final project, the Lantern Pavilion, situated a little up the hillside from the house.

Alison and Peter Smithson died in 1993 and 2003 respectively. Axel Bruchhäuser still lives at Hexenhaus with another Karlchen – his third.

Above: Inside the Hexenhaus, which is filled with the owner's collection of twentieth-century furniture. All the interventions were designed in collaboration with the client.

Opposite: Witch Broom Room – a tiny retreat reached by walkway. It is thought to have been inspired by hide structures in the nearby countryside.

Housing Developments

Alex Ely within the
horseshoe-shaped housing
block that forms the heart
of the Britz Metropolitan
Settlement in Berlin.

Britz Metropolitan Settlement

Location: Berlin, Germany
Architects: Bruno Taut with Martin Wagner
Completed: 1925–30
Chosen by Alex Ely of Mæ Architects

Britz Metropolitan Settlement is simple, utilitarian architecture configured to make a place with a strong identity, designed around how people live. I first visited the development in 1991, before it was listed as a World Heritage Site by UNESCO. When I went again more recently it left a much deeper impression on me and seemed so much more relevant to the work I do now. Maybe as a student I was expecting more, but in many ways it's the quiet expression of the architecture and the careful consideration of the plan and urban layout that makes this so interesting.

I've visited all the six UNESCO-listed estates in Berlin and while they are all interesting, Britz is the one that sticks in the memory because of its variety, richness and cohesion.

Britz is effectively a garden suburb in Berlin. Bruno Taut's design was heavily influenced by Hermann Muthesius who brought Ebenezer Howard's ideas for the English City Movement to Germany along with his reflections on Das Englische Haus. At Britz, these ideas are married with ideals of humane functionalism at a time when there was a huge housing shortage. Co-operatives were formed to build housing for working-class people.

Taut was designing when modernist thinking was pushing against traditional terraces and streets in favour of buildings as abstract objects in landscape, which can be quite alienating. But Taut thought carefully about how people lived, realising that they are more comfortable when there is definition between public and private realms. I like this clear legibility and pursuit of comfort and familiarity.

The urban design is quite straightforward. Apartment buildings create a strong frontage along the main allée, then the scale steps down to two- and three-storey housing. Streets run north-south in rows so kitchens get morning sun and living rooms evening sun. The later phase has terraced housing accessed off footpaths, making it very pedestrian oriented.

I like the way Taut used the buildings to form public spaces and create enclosure. The great set piece is the horseshoe, a dramatic form combined with well-considered landscape and topography with the bowl becoming the curve of the horseshoe with the lake in the middle.

Taut took a simple formula and created a calm architecture with an attention to detail that is hard to achieve in housing these days. Its character is derived from the slight inflection of roads and how the buildings step back slightly to allow the spaces to breathe and create localised amenity. I especially like how at the end of each row of houses, the last house is brought forward to 'bookend' the terrace. The gap behind was plugged by a large street tree. Each street has a different tree specification so they each have their own identity.

Although the housing itself was fairly standard, variety was created with landscape and subtle detailing of fenestrations and colour. Taut controversially believed that colour should have the same rights as form. When Le Corbusier saw Taut's colourful windows he is reported to have claimed "My God, Taut is colour-blind". Five main colours are used in all, but the underlying architecture is robust enough to allow that degree of fluctuation.

There is a very simple articulation with inset rather than projected balconies and glazing above the entrances. The ground floor is raised up slightly to give privacy. The long apartment façades are broken up by brick bonding and the rhythm of the entrances so that they don't appear too monolithic. There's a simplicity, but a richness too, even down to the textured render that catches the light.

A consideration of craft is taken through to the design of the home itself. From the boot scraper by the front door, the draft lobby designed for coats and the paraphernalia of daily life through to well-proportioned rooms focused around ceramic tiled stoves, copious basement storage, kitchens planned with precision and secondary glazing, all contributed to creating desirable and homely dwellings that advanced how people lived at the time.

While there is an economy to its design, the overall modernity of the homes led to political conservatives complaining that they were too opulent for 'simple people'. Britz is still a useful model for placemaking with a generosity in the sense of community it creates between the private spaces. One of the toughest things today in projects that are much denser than Britz is giving houses a sense of individuality while maintaining a calm order.

At Mæ we're also exploring how we can introduce layouts that give something back to the public realm. It might well have been in the back of my mind when designing our housing at the Catford Stadium site with Witherford Watson Mann, where I was thinking about landscape, entrances, framing portals and brick plinths as a means of giving different character to different areas.

It's clear that the people who live at Britz take pride in the place. It's very homely and, with such a mature landscape, it feels like it would be a very good place to live.

Apartment buildings line the main streets in the settlement. Architect Bruno Taut used five basic colours, with corner houses painted white or blue.

BERLIN EXEMPLAR Home to 5,000 Berliners, Britz Metropolitan Settlement was designed by Bruno Taut (1880-1938) for the housing co-operative Gehag of which Taut was chief architect. Taut worked with co-architect and municipal planning head Martin Wagner, and with Leberecht Migge and Ottokar Wagler on the landscape.

The 7.1 ha site was the former Britz manor to the south of the city, and contains 1,285 apartments in blocks rising to three-and-a-half storeys, and 679 largely terraced houses. These were designed in four sizes from 65sq m to 124sq m with many variations in roof line and fenestration. Taut used five basic colours throughout the estate, with the end houses painted in white or blue.

The first phase included a 350m-long horseshoe block around a lake, and was followed by denser phases of more urban character. Democratically, each occupant of the horseshoe apartments had their own area of garden in three rings radiating off the inside of the horseshoe. The development attracted controversy, with the then-radical flat roofs and use of red render seen as a sign of Taut and Gehag's socialist leanings.

Apartment entrance. All the buildings are designed with simple articulation but with a variety of rooflines and details to add individuality to the settlement.

Inside Tautes Heim, a restored museum/rentable house on the Britz estate. The original tiled heater is to the right.

Cany Ash on the roof at Unité d'Habitation, Le Corbusier's pioneering housing development in Marseille.

Unité d'Habitation

Location: Marseille, France

Architect: Le Corbusier

Completed: 1947–52

Chosen by Cany Ash of Ash Sakula Architects

As an architect, visiting the Unité is like coming home. So much of it feels familiar. Yet there's a continuing sense of absolute wonder at how on earth Le Corbusier brought myriad different threads and uses together into this perfect synthesis. It's magic.

This visit is my fourth and I'm sure I'll be back again. I first came 15 years ago with my partner, Robert Sakula and our children but had a long time before been enthused by Peter Carl, my tutor at Cambridge. He was more interested in the symbolism and orphism of Le Corbusier rather than in modularisation, modernity and machinery, and he taught me that you could make your own Corbusian mythology and take from it what you wanted.

The Unité feels like a very special crucible in which people can live, work and play together. It is so much more than the sum of its parts. That first visit was memorable. We encountered it first as tourists; then it seemed as if the building took us in when we made friends with one of the residents as our children played on the roof and she invited us all down to her apartment for lunch. It was fantastic sharing her enthusiasm for the smallest details of her flat – how clever the storage arrangements are in that complicated bit in the middle of the plan that you can never quite get just looking at it on paper, or how thoughtful the variety of alcoves in the stainless-steel splashback behind the sink were.

What's interesting for me is its ambition to be full of ways that people might meet and knit together. It's a complete town in the air – there's the sense of each domain being a very regulated piece that's repeated to make up the façade. You have a double-height and a single-height apartment module that toggle together

beautifully in plan and section. But for such a simple diagram, it feels very complex. It can keep catching you out as you walk around.

Added to this arrangement of apartments are many other uses. There is some very forward social thinking here to lighten the burden of housekeeping – it's maybe what leads the Le Corbusier expert Flora Samuel to call Le Corbusier a feminist. You could drop the kids off in the nursery then have your hair done, go to the shops, go to the gym, commune with nature and the sky on the roof: the ocean liner ideal of lofty individualism and simple community. It very nearly worked. It felt both surreal and straightforwardly obvious to find a working supermarket halfway up the building.

The roof feels like a vast room. People come up to run, walk, to sunbathe or to read. Everyone has their favourite place. In the summer, the pool has water in it and the children come up from the nursery and use the roof as a beach. Residents bring their lunches and the roof acts a hearth or hub for the whole community. Corbusier designed areas for picnic seating and also the 'camel hump' forms for children to play on, which mimic the contours of the landscape so perfectly. There's a lot of light and shadow to play with – it keeps giving. It's difficult to drink it all in. I think of the roofscape as being almost mythically timeless in the generosity of its sculptural forms.

The Unité d'Habitation housed 1,600 people. Le Corbusier started from the big concepts of how people might live together then drilled right down into the detail, which then informs the concept. There is a sense, as I think Le Corbusier puts it, of continually moving from the general to the particular and from the particular back to the general.

When it was built, the Unité was practically in the country and it must have seemed like a brilliant dream to float its immense mass of béton brut above the trees. Unlike the undercrofts of most brutalist buildings that feel so desperate, here there is enough light. These amazing columns that take down the enormous load of the building and conceal the service runs start off massive and then taper to become quite delicate tiptoes before plunging underground, where they spread out again.

Le Corbusier talked most about the dual-aspect, E-type apartment where you enter below and the main bedroom is on a balcony over the living room but its opposite variant with the double-height living room/bedroom and small upstairs entrance/dining room/kitchen also works beautifully. He was interested in having a space with perspectives that are internally dramatic and play with light at different times of day – a fantastic contrast with the perpetual twilight of the corridors. Your eyes can travel and feast – you don't ever feel like you're just staring at the walls and want to get out. In the apartment plans, the two children's rooms seem oddly narrow but in reality they include so much territory inside and out for making things and experimenting, playing, or working. Le Corbusier was interested in letting the clutter of life play with the interior landscape. The original built-in furniture and fittings are amazing – he even designed in a baby-changing table.

It's very fertile – it's hard to think of one of our buildings that hasn't referenced it in some way. We won a competition a few years ago called High Rise to improve a 15-storey tower in Newham and copied the Unité in many ways, in particular the idea of how a building can be a whole town. Our Peabody apartments in

Silvertown have a communal life to them that also owes a lot to the Unité. At the Hothouse art and community centre in Hackney we thought a lot about the Unité when we were creating a sort of shantytown on the roof for artists' live-work studios.

Some of the façade is a bit difficult and new uses need to be found for the empty commercial spaces. But buildings often need reinventing for new audiences. And if, as at the Unité, the architecture is generous and the original programme has vision and ambition, then new life will grow on the old wood.

Above: Twenty-three different apartment configurations were included within the Unité d'Habitation block, as well as shops and community facilities.

Right: A shallow pool on the rooftop. Seating inspired by the contours of the landscape gives views both towards the sea and the surrounding hills.

Unité d'Habitation's distinctive undercroft and pilotis of reinforced béton brut (rough cast) concrete.

CITY BLOCK Unité D'Habitation, Le Corbusier's seminal apartment block in Marseille, is known locally as Maison du Fada (House of the Crazies). Completed in 1952, the 12-storey block was built to house 1,600 people and was famously conceived as a vertical city in the sky, with integral community facilities such as shops, nursery and restaurant.

Commissioned by the French government to deal with the post-war housing shortage, it was the culmination of research by Corbusier into the design of collective housing and use of modular construction techniques. Corbusier devised 23 apartment configurations to cater for varying family sizes, each accessed via internal streets on every third floor. Many of the 337 units are dual aspect with views towards both the Mediterranean and the hillside.

Nearly all the shops in the commercial floor are now shut. Yet residents are fiercely proud of the building, and apartments there are much sought after, particularly by architects.

Unité d'Habitation has been hugely influential on generations of architects. Cany Ash describes it as "a very special crucible where people can live, work and play together."

Adam Khan at the "humane and dignified" public housing of La Tourette near the Vieux Port in Marseille.

La Tourette

Location: Marseille, France

Architect: Fernand Pouillon

Completed: 1948–53

Chosen by Adam Khan of Adam Khan Architects

While the French architect Fernand Pouillon was quite explicit about trying to achieve the monumental, in work such as the La Tourette housing in Marseille this was translated into a very humane and dignified way of making city. He made public housing with a bit of swagger, demonstrating the opposite of the mean-spirited and minimum-necessary approach so prevalent in this type of project.

At the Rue Saint-Laurent, a strong stone arcade is filled with garages and car-repair shops. Broken vehicles and parts spill out of the arcade onto the pavement. Time and wear are evident, and although it is hard to place when this building is from, as you look closely you begin to see a history of additions and changes. Locating a building in architectural history is only one way of sensing a building. Pouillon's housing at Marseille exudes a powerful air of permanence, but one that is highly nuanced. It has the sense of a piece of the city that always existed, but is gently accommodating of change and individual whim.

The arcade is a contemporary stoa, giving the cool shadow and stripy rhythm of shadows, with deep columns that, like a Cistercian abbey, occlude views out but privilege the sensation of light and depth. It contains the ordinary mess of the city – the useful bits that architects find so hard to accommodate well.

Above the arcade a low block of housing forms a terrace, shifting back and forth to create a little tower at the entrance steps and a firmer full-stop tower at the end. The module is consistent but the rhythm of windows skips between wide and narrow. The garish awnings, bulging washing lines and plastic terrace furniture are all subsumed by the monumental presence of the honey-coloured stone

building. String course mouldings of an ogee pattern give a subtle sense of sedimentary build-up and is just enough to give depth and weight to the stone. The control is exquisite and verges on abstraction.

In a subtle way the top floor is treated as an attic, changing tectonic from wall to post and beam. On an upper terrace a plastic greenhouse has filled in the massing. Clearly cheap and ageing rapidly, it finds its place comfortably in the overall picture. This is an architecture of time, able to cope with the wildly varying timescales that are the defining quality of good city.

At the far end of the terrace, where the nineteenth-century buildings survive, is a handsome tower. The stone and the mouldings continue but the openings widen, stretching the stone into a frame grid. There is still a lingering sense of wall, with the vertical and horizontal members too large to be merely a structural frame, the ogee string courses continue at every floor, and the openings have a very considered proportion. As a tower, five bays wide and seven bays deep is a nice proportion, and the 16 storeys keeps everyone in contact with the city ground below.

The floors have an open loggia running round two faces of the tower. Many of these loggias have been filled in with plastic windows. When I visited last this was the exception – it was done unlawfully and the effect was a delightful play of individual improvisation choice within the strong frame of the tower. Now legalised, the process of filling is becoming the norm.

At communal entrances, voluptuous ceramic sculptures sit within a glazed over-scaled doorway. At key moments, a column of

balconies made from oar-shaped timbers form little tower-like accents. A large trellis screen forms a set of loggias to the apartments, and the balustrades are varied slightly across the blocks. This eclectic use of ornament and variation could easily be kitsch but is here well judged.

The flats' plans are simple and the vertical partition walls are flimsy. I can't determine whether this was an intended flexibility in plan, or just expedient. But Pouillon's mastery of cost and building craft enabled the whole project to go ahead when previously stalled. On a very tight budget he made humane housing and city with a sense of generosity. Time pressure is often used as an excuse for the poor housing of the post-war period – but Pouillon ridiculed this, citing his own experience of delivering at great speed.

His motivation was deeper than expediency, it was the desire to define and become a truly modern architect, in a more fundamental way than style. Sensing presciently that the architect's power was slipping away, his fondness for medieval craft led him to try and recover the synthetic, total mastery of the building process that he saw in the ancient architects. This is a pertinent story for our time.

His approach was to integrate the engineering consultants into his own office, forge intimate links with suppliers, buy materials direct and take on more and more of the project management, to become contractor and even investor. It was a time of great opportunity and he was prepared to take risks.

Here at the Vieux Port, the stone facing is a technique called *pierre banchée* using slabs of stone as permanent shuttering. This massively

reduced the material and labour involved in the formwork, and used a local material that was being industrialised by the French government. The result is thrilling, and quite unlike conventional cladding, with a delicious tension between mass and surface lining and with none of the unstable and rootless feeling of a clipped-on façade system.

At many scales the buildings form a frame for the city. Pouillon's housing is part of the post-war reconstruction of the Old Port, the historic centre of Marseille of mainly working-class housing. Pouillon designed many of the buildings and was able to adjust the sensible

but bland masterplan drawn up by the city architect, tweaking heights, positions and issuing sketches to other architects involved.

A montage sketch shows Pouillon testing the height of the tallest tower as seen across the bay. This is accomplished spatial composition, using topography, found condition and techniques of the picturesque to create a calm and lively backdrop for city life.

The monumental is here but is not nostalgic or egocentric. Instead, Pouillon's buildings are a model of relaxed urbanity: generous, strong and accommodating.

Above: Residential court at La Tourette, where architect Fernand Pouillon used slabs of stone as permanent shuttering to speed up construction of the post-war development.

Opposite, left: An arcade is designed to accommodate garages, workshops and other messy bits of the city that architects normally find hard to manage.

Opposite, right: One of the communal entrances in the court at La Tourette. Each has a different coloured ceramic motif set within a glazed over-scaled doorway.

COLOURFUL CHARACTER La Tourette was an early high point in the colourful life and career of Fernand Pouillon (1912–86). Determined to bring high quality to the much-needed, post-war public housing of the time, he built more than 200 apartments as part of La Tourette, including a 21-storey tower block, all achieved on a low budget with the help of organisational and technical innovations.

He worked on further low-cost housing in Algeria and Iran before being jailed for his alleged role on a housing project on the outskirts of Paris in 1961. He escaped from jail and was eventually acquitted of the original crime but jailed again for escaping.

After his release he worked extensively in Algeria, designing more than 30 hotels between 1964–84. He was pardoned in 1971 and returned to France in 1972.

Julian Lewis at the piazza
lined with shops within
the 1960 Olympic village
in Rome.

1960 Rome Olympic Village

Location: Flaminio district, Rome, Italy

Architects: Vittorio Cafiero, Adalberto Libera, Luigi Moretti, Vincenzo Monaco, Amedeo Luccichenti

Completed: 1958–60

Chosen by Julian Lewis of East Architects

At East, we're drawn to fringe areas of the city where there is less urban clarity but plenty of potential. Perhaps that's why I'm so intrigued by this part of Rome – the site of the 1960 Olympic Village in Flaminio. It might not be among the textbook architectural highlights of the city, but there is so much to learn from here in terms of urban place-making.

I first became aware of it many years ago when my English teacher at school gave me a book on Pier Luigi Nervi, engineer of several of the site's structures including the viaduct that runs through the village. Then, around 15 years ago, I visited the Olympic Village, and realised how close Nervi's stadium and viaduct were to the Olympic housing. I felt a real convergence between the epic set-piece nature of the stadiums and viaduct and the naturalness of the housing.

This difficult balance between something that's background and something that's carefully placed for impact is one of the reasons I keep coming back. The stadiums are carefully mixed into the overall landscape and work far better than they do at the London Olympic site in Stratford, where all the buildings are trying to be special events.

The Rome Olympic Village suggests an attitude towards housing that was all about responding to a place rather than a site. One of the interesting things about it is the difficulty of clarifying authorship. It was designed by a group of architects including Luigi Moretti and Adalberto Libera but I still don't really know who did what. You get the idea that they were great collaborators.

On my first visit, I was excited by the strong, clear geometry of the housing. Long thin strips of buildings seem to walk into the landscape. What's particularly lovely is the way the viaduct and the housing relate to each other spatially and materially. The viaduct was built to help transport people to the site and, because it was elevated, allowed the landscape of the village to flow continuously underneath.

One of the qualities of the housing is that it isn't overdesigned. Housing in Britain often tends to stake its place in the urban setting stridently excluding the existing qualities of the place, but this takes a back step formally while still creating an identity through its use of materials. You would not call this an estate, or street, or even courtyards. These are fields of houses set into a wild parkland edge. It makes a wild edge of Rome into a place. You can walk through it.

These architects were looking at how to locate architecture and how to locate generosity. They understood that architecture can't be at play everywhere. If it was, the result would be too explosive. Instead, they added to the place gently. Put together, the effect might not be sculptural but it is powerfully spatial.

Instead of the buildings occupying the spaces, the housing makes the spaces. Some blocks make tight spaces that are quite charged while others are slacker – the character of the area changes radically when the blocks are placed closer together. I particularly like the criss-cross patterned piazza lined with shops, which is like a stretched version of Michelangelo's Piazza del Campidoglio. It's incredibly effective in how it just flexes inwards rather than going for a big heroic gesture.

The viaduct's structure recalls the columned bases of the housing and offers space for the imagination. I find it genuinely exciting to have such a highly determined area – the housing – next to the undetermined space underneath the viaduct. Whenever I bring students out here this always prompts a discussion about the nature of prescribed and unprescribed use. They are usually rather bewildered because there is nothing specific to look at.

On the other side of the viaduct, the blocks are arranged at right angles as if they are moving towards the viaduct rather than alongside it. Then, further away, there are the cross-shaped blocks, which, put together, start to hold together courtyards. Ungated, even these more formal spaces are dynamically engaged with the wider place, enlivening the experience of the moving pedestrian.

The inspiring thing for me is the village's uncompromising nature but at the same time its softness – its scale is all very human. I like how you can look around and can't quite see where the centre of the village is – this is not a highly regimented space. As you walk around, the arrangement seems a little chaotic, but I find it quite spellbinding.

There is a lot of instinct involved and a painterly quality. The architects have managed to mix in a personal judgement of materials quite unlike the fascist architecture of the Mussolini era. The pilotis supporting the housing blocks are delicate and have been designed with facets that catch the light. The architects use the same brick throughout but in some of the buildings the bricks run vertically, and in others they run horizontally – they are seeded from one building type into the other.

At the corner of the Type A blocks, the concrete bands step down and become lintels. They look

papery – snipped and cut at the corner as if the architect was tailoring clothes. You sense this massive structure beneath this delicate brick 'wallpaper'. I also like the blank ends to the blocks which read as extrusions; the strange baskets on top of the roofs of some of the housing that hide the services; and the way the really flat wide facades of the horizontal blocks mirror the generosity of a deeply spatial park landscape.

The Olympic Village was an example of how the energy and big vision of modernism could work in conjunction with the existing city. Although at East we are careful to avoid overdesigning our buildings, and sensitive to working alongside existing qualities of place, it is also inspiring to see the scale and ambition of a place like the Olympic Village where confidence and architectural rigour were crucial in making the place amazing.

Parallel housing blocks – Julian Lewis admires the uncompromising nature of the Olympic village.

More than half a century on, the Olympic housing is surrounded by a mature park setting.

GAMES LEGACY The 1960 Olympic Village was a showpiece post-war project for Rome, containing housing for 6,500 people as well as the sporting facilities themselves.

It was built to the north of the city in the Flaminio district, and was the first time the Olympics were used as a catalyst for urban change. Its architects included Luigi Moretti and Adalberto Libera. Engineer Pier Luigi Nervi designed the two indoor sports arenas PalaLottomatica and Palazzetto dello Sport, the outdoor stadium, and the Corso di Francia viaduct, which runs through the middle of the village, and divided the housing for male athletes from that for the female athletes. It is elevated on T-shaped piers to allow free passage across the site.

After the Olympics, the apartments were used as public housing, but the area declined during the seventies and eighties, and the space beneath the viaduct remains underused.

Greg Penoyre on the roof
of Great Arthur House,
the tallest building on the
Golden Lane Estate.

Golden Lane Estate

Location: London, UK
Architect: Chamberlin, Powell & Bon
Completed: 1952–62
Chosen by Greg Penoyre of Penoyre & Prasad

Golden Lane is pretty special to me. It's a very civilised place, rare in early post-war housing.

I worked for Chamberlin, Powell & Bon on the Barbican between 1977–80, during which time I got to know their work in some detail. They had fantastic photographs of the early projects, including the evolution of Golden Lane Estate, and over the years as I found out more, this became an important project for me. After site visits to the Barbican I used to go up to the roof garden on the top of Great Arthur House and have my lunch looking out over the estate and the whole of London.

Golden Lane was the result of an architectural competition, after the City of London decided it needed new housing in the bomb-damaged city fringes. Peter Chamberlin, Geoffry Powell and Christoph Bon decided to enter separately to maximise their chances of winning, with an agreement to set up in practice together if any of them did. Powell, perhaps the most intuitive designer, won it. He was in his early 30s and it was a great opportunity for a young architect.

I find it particularly interesting that although the architects were determinedly formalistic, they were also so interested in detail. And Golden Lane is all about the details, the spaces and how people live. It was a highly sensitive way of designing. They thought of it as a whole: the urban spaces were as important as the flats, full of very civilised moments such as the little group of seats and trees near the community centre, one of my favourites.

They were designing a bit of city – not just housing. Powell said there was no attempt at the informal but the result is much more humane than that might sound. Powell's scheme was initially for five low blocks and

a tower but this evolved and grew. The three partners divided it up to detail with quite different languages. Chamberlin did Great Arthur House, Powell designed Stanley Cohen House, using pick-hammered concrete and Bon did the detailing on Bayer House. They weren't seeking to unify. It was the first time they had come together as a practice and they were clearly still finding their feet.

What I really love is how the estate represents a time that contrasts with how we work now. They had the freedom to explore their architectural aesthetic and there is a clear evolution from the relative simplicity of form in the early 1950s to the much more figured, late-Corbusian expression of the subsequent buildings, a language they explored more wholeheartedly in the Barbican eight years later. They were also curious about different construction techniques and on Golden Lane seemed to have freedom to experiment.

The highest element at Golden Lane is Great Arthur House, a symmetrical building with an asymmetric composition at roof level, which is four flats across, each single-bedroom and single-aspect. Chamberlin decided halfway through the design that it would be better to have something exciting at the top and designed a great flourish, giving it the beautiful sailing roof that soars over the whole estate, becoming its defining characteristic. I'm sure they'd been to Marseille – everyone was looking to Corbusier at the time – and Chamberlin may well have come back from seeing the Unité (see pp 144–149) saying "I want one of those" and added one to the roof.

But Chamberlin, Powell and Bon were viewed as outsiders – expressionist, undisciplined and wilful. Powell used to say that nobody

liked their work. They were almost seen as decorative but I think they were just interested in richness and detail.

Something has really worked here in terms of public space. There's a subtlety of layers. The relationship between private and public is blurred by devices such as the steps down into the courtyard at Bayer House, where a series of flights separate the public garden from the podium and the flats themselves. They were well-educated and knew about the great courtyards of the world. They also drew on ideas such as Vermeer and Pieter de Hooch's observations of thresholds, and from the treatment of the outdoors in Indian gardens and Renaissance architecture.

This brings a much richer treatment to a very simple scheme, and the way they manipulated landscape is one of the things that makes the atmosphere at Golden Lane so special. Much of it anticipates the Barbican, such as the idea of the water going right up to the buildings and the use of stepping stones both at ground level and in the roof garden at Great Arthur House.

At Penoyre & Prasad, the architecture we pursue is about how people inhabit space and how architecture interacts with the human experience. There's a real pleasure in ordinary circumstance. I learnt much about this from my time at Chamberlin Powell & Bon and from Golden Lane. I also learnt about detail, in particular making one element perform more than one function and so become indispensable in the architecture as a whole.

It is a pleasure to spend time here. Golden Lane Estate is on my doorstep and I see it and the Barbican from my office. It is valuable to remember why it is so special.

CITY SLICKER Widely regarded as an exemplar of British modernism, Golden Lane Estate consists of 557 flats and maisonettes and is listed Grade II and Grade II* (Crescent House).

Built by the City of London in Blitz-devastated Cripplegate, it was conceived as council housing for single people and couples.

Geoffry Powell won a competition for the commission in 1952, and set up in practice with Christoph Bon and Peter Chamberlin to develop the project. Their Corbusier-inspired design rejected the traditional urban form of houses on streets for a mixed-use estate of eight low-to-medium-rise blocks dominated by the 16-storey Great Arthur House, the first residential tower block in London over 50m in height.

Over the project's 10-year duration, the architectural style of the estate evolved. The 1962 Crescent Building on Goswell Road, the last to be completed, is closest in style to the adjacent Barbican Estate, which Chamberlin, Powell & Bon went on to design.

Above: Basterfield House elevation. Architect Chamberlin, Powell & Bon paid great attention to the landscape around the housing blocks to create what Greg Penoyre calls a 'very civilised place'

Right: Topped with a sailing roof flourish, Great Arthur House (right) towers over eight lower blocks on the Golden Lane Estate.

Peter St John in the arcade at Aldo Rossi's "quiet and powerful" Gallaratese housing in Milan.

Gallaratese

Location: Milan, Italy
Architect: Aldo Rossi
Completed: 1969–73

Chosen by Peter St John of Caruso St John Architects

I love the modern architecture of Milan and could show you many elegant buildings there that are more beautiful than Aldo Rossi's project at the Gallaratese. But if I was to choose one that has affected me most it would be this one. As an architect your feelings about architecture are formed when you are young. You find themes and ideals then, and if you are persistent and fortunate you will realise them later in life.

I visited this building when I was 20, which is an impressionable age, and it was the moment I first felt what was interesting in classicism, and how it was possible to do a piece of modern architecture with classical themes. I was at the end of my degree at the Bartlett in 1980 and about to enter the AA for my diploma. I had visited the first Architecture Biennale in Venice, the Presence of the Past, curated by Paolo Portoghesi, and then went on to Milan to see the Gallaratese. It was way out of the centre of the city in a modern suburb. I was on my own and it wasn't easy to find. The building is about 200m long and is raised up on tall legs. Underneath is an arcade which extends from the street into the centre of the estate, leading to other buildings.

It was hot and the wide piers along the arcade cast a sharp shadow off into the distance. At the mid-point, there was a sort of interruption of shapes in the light, a massive rise of steps and some big, round columns. Everything was painted an ivory colour. I can remember that a few people shuffled across this monumental empty space while I was looking – a woman with some shopping, a few children – appearing and disappearing. There was an echo of steps. The atmosphere was heightened like on a stage and it was dramatic, but not in a rhetorical way as it was somehow also tender to the figures.

It felt as if all Italy was there: its grandeur and its poverty, its monuments and its ruins. It was moving that such concrete simplicity could hold such allusions.

The whole building is relentlessly basic and singular in its concept. The flats are arranged between parallel walls above the arcade on two and three floors with deck access. The facade of the flats facing a modest park is a row of big square holes in the white wall, with the further subdivisions of the frames in green and with recessed balconies, so that although there is a lot of repetition, there is also a lot of depth and shadow, as if the structure is an empty shell. At the centre of the length at a change in level, there is a break and the round columns, as if older fragments from another, bigger building have been embedded in the facade.

Rossi had the idea that buildings should show the passage of time. He was interested in the form of the city and how its monuments gave it identity. His forms were always very basic, coming from recognisable roots or typologies, but overlaid with the imagination of the architect. He argued that buildings should be general in their form and non-specific about their function, because if they last their use will change over time.

There is certainly none of the complexity that is expected to give social housing a domestic scale. But there is generosity and a public scale which brings a grandness to the everyday. You also think of aqueducts and amphitheatres, how their horizontality and scale gives definition to a topography, and what it might be like to live on a bridge with its open views.

I'd seen these things in Rossi's manifesto, *The Architecture of the City*, and understood better

what he meant when I felt the monumental presence of this building. At that time, the idea of looking to architectural history for models was new, and also completely different from the open-ended empiricism of my architectural education. Of course this was to continue.

But seeing this quiet and powerful building at that time feels like it had a lasting effect. Rossi's *A Scientific Autobiography* remains for me the most beautiful and convincing writing by an architect. Rossi led me to appreciate different and particular architectures that were around when we started our practice: the Half Moon Theatre by Florian Beigel (through whose office I met my partner Adam Caruso); the work of Tony Fretton; and the early projects of Jacques Herzog and Pierre de Meuron (who were taught by Rossi) that were innovatively built yet rather ancient in character.

There are influences in our work, more in ideas and mood than in appearance. There is often an interest in the monumental scale, but also in the city and its ordinary, background buildings, which Rossi writes about, and which were an anathema to modernist architects, who wanted everything to be new and different. There's always something familiar in our work too, often when we are working with existing buildings or fragments and are looking for some continuity in the design to ease the distinction between old and new.

It was Rossi who said that his basic principle was to persistently hold to only one theme. I think it is true that deep down you're always doing the same project, just with improving skill and in different circumstances. The long journey to realise a building consistently in all its details is easily as difficult as the months of making the initial design. Years later, people will appreciate

its lasting quality if it is done well, even if they are using it quite differently from how you intended.

Revisiting the Gallaratese, the place feels more charming than before. The landscape has matured, people have occupied the walkways with their plants in a way that feels settled, and there is an ugly suspended ceiling in the arcade. But it still has this melancholic, monumental quality that made such an impression on me 30 years ago.

Above: Rossi's Gallaratese housing block stretches 200 metres and overlooks a mature communal landscape. Apartments are dual-aspect.

Opposite: An imposing arcade runs the length of the Gallaratese. Peter St John appreciates the way the public scale gives a "grandness to the everyday".

MILAN MONUMENTAL The Gallaratese housing block helped make the reputation of Aldo Rossi (1931–1997). Built in a newly established suburb in the north west of Milan, the housing is the fifth element within a larger 440-unit complex designed by Carlo Aymonino.

Reached via a piazza within one of Aymonino's buildings, Rossi's housing is a 200m-long, rectangular block of gallery-accessed flats arranged above a ground-floor arcade. Each dual-aspect apartment has a covered balcony and overlooks the communal garden or a piazza.

According to Rossi, the form was a reference to the galleried *ballatoio* housing of Milan of the 1920s. Plans for the arcade to contain shops were unfulfilled. Initially open to the surrounding townscape, the complex has latterly been fenced in with concierges controlling access. As a consequence perhaps, it appears well-kept and free of graffiti and litter.

Piers Gough at The Barbican in the City of London. The complex's baroque confidence has greatly influenced his own work as an architect.

The Barbican

Location: City of London, London, UK
Architect: Chamberlin, Powell & Bon
Completed: 1982
Chosen by Piers Gough of CZWG

When I first went to the Architectural Association in the mid-1960s the big London buildings of the era were the Post Office Tower; Centre Point going up another floor every night to become famous for being empty; the beautifully elegant Economist complex (see pp 24–29) worshipped by architects and planners; the Queen Elizabeth Hall and the Hayward with their concrete guts on the outside; and the Barbican.

Of these the Barbican was the most mysterious and magnificent. A mauve brick-walled citadel enclosing three spectacularly powerful residential towers with lower office slabs arranged on either side of a brief section of super highway prosaically named London Wall. The Barbican was heroic and gutsy, the quintessence of brutalism in finishes but with the curves and sectional cleverness of [American late-modernist architect] Paul Rudolph surrounding lush landscapes.

Elia Zenghelis, later to start OMA with Rem Koolhaas, was our first-year master at the AA and turned us on to Russian constructivism, and then Rudolph and all things heroic. Elia was particularly fascinated by the possibilities inherent in three-dimensional cities suggested by the drawings of his almost namesake Antonio Sant'Elia. Meanwhile the fifth year was presided over by Peter Cook and Archigram. The three-dimensional city was rampantly celebrated with not just elevated roads and pedestrian levels but mini people movers at all altitudes and angles. Buildings were skeletal with plug-in accommodation all in fluorescent colours, fabulously pop.

The Barbican, with its multi-levels of pedestrian realm, was the closest built reality to the seemingly inevitable three-dimensional complexity of the future city. For me it was exciting that this new world was starting in London. City authorities even planned to retrofit an upper level 'pedway' system around the existing streets.

The most exhilarating thing about the Barbican is the sheer scale of its ambition and that they actually got the whole damn thing finished. This is a much rarer event today. It is a complete work conceived and executed by one practice – such a contrast to today with our fussy need for a restless variety of architects.

This confidence reminds me what it was like in the sixties when architects were confident and respected. We were all going to build and change the world. I find it dispiriting that now when they are building these new cities in China and the Gulf, they aren't attempting the three dimensional multi-level city but just pompous boulevards and avenues à la nineteenth century Paris with bigger separate buildings on them.

The Barbican is a three-dimensional jigsaw. Here, you don't know where the ground level is. It's all about buildings and landscape interlocking. You look up, you look down, you look sideways and they all have a convincing claim to be the effective terra firma.

The total effect is that the buildings don't so much stand as meld into various levels of landscape. And what landscapes – the squares are some of the most handsome in London with the bonus of public pedestrian spaces and routes overlooking them, and the unique lake.

Chamberlin Powell & Bon were very skilful scenographers as well as bloody strong architects – there is a fantastic curved bit around the sculpture court. And along the top of the lower-rise blocks there are almost Moorish shell roofs. There's something very wonderful and playful about it. The architects certainly weren't parsimonious with their style. They were in the great tradition of bloody-minded English baroque from Vanbrugh via Nash to this. This is the greatest work of twentieth-century baroque architecture.

The Barbican has this sheer physical joy – what architecture can do with long horizontal buildings combined with tall vertical ones. I still think these are the most handsome residential buildings in London. The horizontal ones are the quintessence of horizontality and repetition, with the verticality of the towers equally emphasised. There's something about the three towers – so smouldering and craggy, and darkly dramatic. They are the most elemental habitations, the generosity of the balconies clear in the idiosyncratic silhouettes.

At the centre, around the lake, this spectacular space is seemingly strongly defined by the horizontal buildings but also segues into other overlapping spaces: the church of St Giles Cripplegate; the City of London Girls School dropping sheer into the water like a protective moat; the arts-centre restaurants spilling out on to southfacing terraces; the sunken gardens in the lake itself. Then, in the most outrageously brilliant piece of theatre, a building on a massive colonnade blithely crosses the centre of the space with a public bridge/walkway suspended below between the pilotis. Sublime.

Of course, all this concrete won't be to everyone's architectural taste but it is bloody well done. The bush-hammered stuff is amazing – you can see where the point of the hammer went in. Yes, it's a bit dirty. But it's a piece of craftwork.

Now it's nearly 50 years old and I think it has aged brilliantly.

The arts centre part of the complex came later and was famously compromised by being shoehorned in, but I have a great fondness for the complexity in its interior matching that of the outside. Some of the interior materials are terrific. The golden brass handrails give a suitably glamorous bling to the Piranesian spaces. The drama of the tapering theatre access stairs is particularly enhanced by the brass handrails, arranged crossways like the starting stalls of a racecourse.

The two things that have given the Barbican a bad reputation are the hellish street tunnel of Beech Street and not being able to find the upper walkway level. The criticism is a bit off because we expect and enjoy getting lost in cities and finding unexpected routes and vistas. The Barbican has these in spades.

Its biggest influence has been to be confident of strong architecture. It gives me the inspiration to design buildings that are exciting-looking without trying to be icons, and that solidity can be just as modern as lightweight buildings. Also the Barbican taught me not to

worry about being of your time. It's inevitable, but buildings can also be timeless in appeal and magnificence. It's there as a challenge to do idiosyncratic, exciting even baroque buildings at every opportunity.

Even when I am rushing late for a film, I think the Barbican is so phenomenal, so amazing. It's such a pity there aren't more like it.

Above: Foyer inside the Barbican Arts Centre, whose interior complexity matches that of the external complex.

Opposite: The Barbican's central public court, with lakeside terraces and sunken gardens. To the left the lake is crossed by an apartment block raised on pilotis with a walkway suspended underneath.

BAROQUE CITADEL Built on a Second World War bomb site, the Barbican had a long and torturous gestation.

Planning for a residential district including schools and gardens began in the early 1950s and by the 1960s it was decided to add an arts centre, all designed by Chamberlin, Powell & Bon. It was eventually approved by the City of London's Court of Common Council, after its longest sitting on record debating whether or not to proceed.

Wayfinding through the complex has been a persistent problem, not helped by the late integration of the arts centre into the design of the complex. Another factor was the discontinuation of the Corporation of London's plans for a series of walkways linking buildings above street level. New signage was introduced as part of an extensive refurbishment of the arts centre by Allford Hall Monaghan Morris in 2007. The complex was Grade II listed in 2001.

Byker Estate

Location: Newcastle, UK
Architect: Ralph Erskine
Completed: 1969–83
Chosen by Sarah Featherstone of Featherstone Young

I stumbled across the Byker Estate when I was studying at Kingston. Our professors were more interested in modernism in its purest form – Mies, Corbusier – and the follow-on generation like the Smithsons and Rossi. Ralph Erskine seemed to be doing something a little different to this school of thinking, demonstrating a more humane approach that interested me. Instead of being constrained by formalistic theories of architecture as object, he seemed more concerned with people and process. Engaging with communities gave him direction.

Byker intrigued me, although I didn't get to visit until the end of the 1990s when it was quite run down and in parts felt scary to be walking around. Even then, though, the way he had choreographed the streets and public spaces and his eye for everyday details made me feel both comfortable and exhilarated. You could see that Erskine had taken a real delight in the design and planning of the estate.

At the time there was a backlash against slum-clearance programmes, and Erskine was brought in to design the Byker redevelopment because he was known for his more socially responsive approach. He and his team set up shop within 'old' Byker, and some of his colleagues even lived in the old Tyneside terraced housing so they could get under the skin of the place and find out more about what people wanted.

Erskine's approach was pretty experimental – he didn't start off with a masterplan but with a 'plan of intent' to create a new neighbourhood by collaborating with the residents on its design. An early achievement was to stop wholesale demolition that would destroy the community spirit. Instead, he proposed phased development with families still living in their old house until their new one was built.

The result was nothing like the monolithic, repetitive and relentless housing blocks that replaced many of the slums at that time. Instead, Erskine managed to retain a high density through a range of building heights from one to 13 storeys. There is a huge sense of variety, with numerous different house typologies. He broke with the more rigid grid street pattern that the older terraced housing had followed down the very steep hill, by cutting new paths and streets across it to work better with the topography. He introduced a hierarchy of streets and courts around which clusters of houses and flats were arranged to form smaller neighbourhoods. He often linked these clusters to one of the original community buildings that he felt should be retained as familiar landmarks, like St Lawrence Church and Shipley Baths.

Interestingly, the highest building is not Byker Wall but the sheltered housing of Tom Collins House – which I love, given that you normally associate this kind of housing with low-rise buildings but here it is the older folk who get the great views over the city.

Originally there was going to be a motorway running along the northern edge; this was one of the reasons for the infamous Byker Wall element, as it would provide an acoustic barrier to the traffic. But Erskine was also interested in using this buffer-wall concept to create a microclimate within the estate to protect it from the icy North Sea winds. The wall is pretty big and, with only small windows to the north, could have seemed relentless. But Erskine breaks the scale down by varying the height and profile of the roof, which soars up and down, and by playing with the brick patterning. This gets more pronounced over the gateways, which appear like gaps in a traditional city wall

Sarah Featherstone at the south side of Byker Wall as she revisits the "surprisingly picturesque" Byker Estate in Newcastle.

171

and seem to almost trace the pattern of the houses abutting it on the inside.

In the end the motorway didn't happen, but the wall is not the white elephant some say it is as it still blocks out the traffic noise and provides a climate that seems to have nurtured some very healthy-looking trees and some quite exotic planting.

To many, what makes Byker visually striking is the wall and the brightly coloured housing it encircles. But for me, it's also the variety and the attention to detail. These little touches – ventilation shafts doubling up as bird-boxes, plant-boxes on top of bin stores and the curious salvaged city ruins such as cobbles and ornaments from the old Byker – create touchstones to the past, and speak volumes to the locals. All bring a more human scale and a delight in the everyday.

Byker is lively and stimulating. Helped by the sloping topography, Erskine plays with scale and height to break up potential monotony; he frames views, squeezes space and then opens it out. There's almost an Italian hill-town quality to some parts, and I love that he reworks familiar local features such as the traditional ginnel passageway. Getting a little lost at Byker feels like a good thing as it is always shortly followed by the comfort of finding a familiar landmark around the next corner.

To me Byker is surprisingly picturesque and has an English eccentricity about it. But for many, Erskine's architecture is dismissed as whimsy and folksy. And these are not the only criticisms of Byker. There were a lot of good intentions to retain the original community but this didn't happen as much as they hoped and later it became very much a council dumping ground. By and large these are not

the faults of the architecture, but social failings symptomatic of the political climate and sadly common to many UK estates. And yet what has come out of these problems is the estate's ability to adapt, which is one of its successes. There is a looseness in the buildings and a deliberate ambiguity to the use of some spaces, which allows people to appropriate them and make them their own. I'm not sure what Erskine would think of the recent listing, which instigated with good intention to stop demolition of key buildings, has perhaps inhibited people from being able to adapt their own homes and gardens.

Erskine was way ahead of his time – many of the ideas he was experimenting with at Byker are only now coming to the fore. His style of architecture isn't everyone's cup of tea but his social agenda and attention to the everyday have had a lasting influence.

Above: Walkways give permeability through the vast estate and reference the ginnels of the terraced housing it replaced.

Opposite: The famous Byker Wall contains 620 maisonettes and was conceived as an acoustic barrier against a proposed but unrealised motorway.

COMMUNITY ENGAGEMENT Northumberland-born Ralph Erskine (1914-2005) was an early proponent of community architecture, favouring extensive consultation and collaboration with residents. He spent most of his working life in Sweden and the 81ha Byker Estate is his best-known UK work, built on the site of Victorian back-to-back terrace housing to the east of the city centre. Its bright colours and quirky touches were a break with some of the more technocratic social housing of the time.

Before redevelopment, the Byker ward housed more than 13,000 people. After the estate was built, there were 9,000 in more than 2,000 units. Although largely two-storey, the estate is best-known for its 10-storey 'shield' of Byker Wall, which contains 620 maisonettes. Erskine apparently modelled it on Arctic housing in Sweden.

The vast majority of Erskine's proposals were built between 1969 and 1983. By the late 1990s, Byker had become perceived as a problem estate. Since then, it has been widely refurbished, although many of the original shops are now shut. It was Grade II* listed in 2007. It is now owned by the Byker Community Trust.

Above: Vivid brick patterning indicates a route through Byker Wall into the estate beyond.

Right: The blue roof of Tom Collins House. The sheltered housing block is the highest structure on the estate.

Gerard Maccreanor in
the courtyard of Piraeus,
a residential development
in the former docklands
of Amsterdam.

Piraeus

Location: KNSM island, Amsterdam, The Netherlands
Architect: Hans Kollhoff with Christian Rapp
Completed: 1989–94
Chosen by Gerard Maccreanor of Maccreanor Lavington

Richard [Lavington] was interested in the work of Hans Kollhoff and so we visited the Piraeus building in Amsterdam when it was completed in 1994. We were excited by it – not because of its rather unusual shape, but because it related to an ongoing conversation we were having about what a building can be, and how appearance can touch upon things to do with character and disposition. Kollhoff talks about the tectonic, about the way a building's appearance refers to its underlying structural system. He also refers to a building's "demeanour" and its "character" and the idea of civicness – these are all notions we like to discuss in our office.

It's hard to imagine it now, but when we first visited Piraeus, it was one of the only buildings on the island. It sat here, a nostalgic reference to the warehouses that used to line the river yet also part of a modern rebuilding of the city. Piraeus feels a lot older than it is and that's a theme we like to use in our work.

Often in a large development where the market is untested and regeneration goes in phases there's a temptation to start with the cheap buildings. But on this island Piraeus was the first building to be built and it is of the highest quality – many things are handmade. This extra quality was funded by the municipality, which recognised that the first sets the tone for what follows. In 2003, when we designed the Ijburg Blok 4 housing in Amsterdam, our building followed a similar path.

Piraeus is not stylistically traditional but it is continually referencing the past. Many Dutch critics who are uncomfortable with discussing tradition emphasise the continuous folded form and describe the building as iconic, but Kollhoff is interested in more sophisticated concepts than form alone. The folded form is only a mechanism to achieve the desired tectonic expression. The result is object-like and has a strong presence but Kollhoff wouldn't describe it as iconic. The building is in fact rather quiet and unassuming, a sort of gentle giant relaxing on the quay side.

The building does not display its precise function. When you stand in front of it, it's hard to tell whether it's for living or working. Instead, its role is to be a container of different uses and typologies. This lack of representation of the use is something we have explored too, a search for neutrality that invites the unexpected.

The height of the doors is fantastic and they are also very decorative – when you enter it, you know you live in a very beautiful building. One of the influences we took from Piraeus is that even though it's a simple building, it still deals with decoration. The idea that you could decorate a building was not at all fashionable in the nineties, and in this sense the design ignored the trends of the time in favour of a resolute pursuit of purpose. In this way I think it was well ahead of its time.

Piraeus has an enormous number of different apartment typologies, 56 in total, and that's one of the things that makes this building so successful. It attracts a huge variety of people, all with different needs and demands. The building seems to house all the differences you find in the street, and this variety makes it part of the street, and a part of the city.

Piraeus deals with the border between public and private in a very clear way. There is no 'in-between' realm. All the entrances are clearly visible on the outside of the building and the ground-floor elevations are either filled with cafés, retail units or simply left as blank brick walls. The blank walls, far from being a problem, save the building from that typical commercial plinth, yet do not reduce the activity around the building. Dutch residential architecture handles the relationship between the building and the public space extremely well. Municipalities, supervisors and the Welstand – the equivalent of design review panels – all work very hard to make sure the environment around the building works. This social concern was in its infancy in the nineties, and Piraeus very much led the way.

I think the Passages artwork on the west elevation is a fantastic addition. Too often the relationship between artist and architect doesn't work and the building gets an incongruous add-on, but here it does. The artwork really reacts with the adjacent public space, even more so in the evening when the panels are illuminated and a mysterious warm light emanates from the building. Everything about the building priortises public space. There are no empty gestures.

The Piraeus building along with our Zaaneiland European housing were among the first projects that recognised brick as the traditional Dutch building material and they were discussed together for their brickness. By the early 1990s, Dutch architects favoured concrete and stucco, flat roofs and a decidedly modernist appearance instead. Today, almost all clients say they want a brick building because it weathers well and ages gracefully. It's interesting that it was two foreign architects who reinstated its use.

When I came back to visit the building, it did not disappoint. It has an undefined timelessness that is reassuring for a chronophobic like me, and it gives me a sense of place – in time.

DOCKLANDS REVIVAL Piraeus is a housing development built on KNSM island as part of the regeneration of Amsterdam's north-eastern port area. The island was one of several artificial peninsulas built between 1874 and 1924 for passenger and cargo ships. The Piraeus site – a reference to Greek-Dutch trading links – was situated along the southern edge of the island and included a 1920s three-storey building, which had to be retained.

German architect Hans Kollhoff created a monolithic block with two courtyards, which wraps itself behind the existing building and then returns to carry on along the waterfront. Away from the waterfront, the building rises to nine storeys, but on the south elevation it folds down from six storeys to four storeys. The west end is cut away to create Passages, a four-storey high colonnade designed by Dutch artist Arno van der Mark.

The development, once nicknamed the Dark Dinosaur, is now widely seen as an exemplar of waterfront building.

Left: Communal entrance, with decoratively arranged letter boxes. "When you enter it, you know you live in a very beautiful building," says Gerard Maccreanor.

Right: Passages, a four-storey high colonnade designed at the west end of Pireaus by artist Arno van der Mark. Apartments overlook a communal garden.

Places of Worship

David Archer inside the Steinhof Church in Vienna, which was an inspiration for his practice's design of the Sans Souci hotel in the same city.

Steinhof Church

Location: Vienna, Austria

Architect: Otto Wagner

Completed: 1904–07

Chosen by David Archer of Archer Humphryes Architects

I first came across this church in books when I was curiously exploring different expressions of architecture in the early 1980s.

At the time there was a surge of interest in arts and crafts amid a backlash against brutalism and abstract concrete structures. That sort of thing wasn't remotely on the agenda when I studied at Canterbury and the Bartlett, but much later I came to Vienna for work and finally visited the Steinhof church for myself as I worked my way through the architectural riches of the city.

Julie Humphryes and I at Archer Humphryes were designing a hotel and there seemed to us to be no better point of departure when creating a contemporary Viennese interior than this incredibly beautiful church. It forms the focus of a mental asylum which its architect, Otto Wagner, designed at the same time as his other seminal Vienna building, the Post Office Savings Bank. While the site was located on the outskirts of the city, those living there had a position of privilege looking out over the city and enjoying the woodland setting. And by giving it a gold dome and positioning it classically on top of the hill, Wagner made the church a landmark over all Vienna. The entirety is a symbol of Vienna as a progressive city of the twentieth century.

The approach is highly managed for what is in effect a spiritual journey, passing through the gates to the sanitorium, then up through the woods to the church at the summit.

Formally, it doesn't break any new ground in terms of shape or character although the fixings of the marble slabs are interesting as an expression of cladding rather than load-bearing walls. But this is incidental – the real beauty of the church is in its interior.

Here, within this classically static, centrally planned church, there is the idea of the complete artistic environment, with Wagner commissioning all of the many artists involved, and the decoration envisaged as a direct expression of the celestial.

It was very modern and overwhelmingly white with light-gold tracery and worked through with a modern abstract decoration. I think there are resonances with Whistler, who had been exploring white on white in his Symphony in White paintings. To us now, the overall effect seems opulent and quite decadent. Yet at the time the Steinhof church was considered to be a relatively sparse, abstract space.

What most appeals to me is that the decoration is born out of the construction of the space, which makes it all the more modern. There is an emphasis on the vertical that takes you up through several bands of horizontal layering from the decorative floor tiling, marble lower walls and fluted plaster above, with the relief of the plaster catching the light.

The inside of the dome is carefully designed to accommodate a rectilinear pattern, with panels of fluting in every other square. As you look around, you find drama incidentally in the decoration. I particularly like the four pendant lights, which are designed like dripping gold as if coming down to earth from heaven.

The altar and the pulpit are more extreme in decoration, and the eye is drawn to them by Gustav Klimt-like abstract swirls and florals. The stained-glass windows have abstracted geometric blue triangles worked into the glass and there are stylised flowers akin to that of Charles Rennie Mackintosh's work at the Glasgow School of Art (pp46–51).

It's also very practical for the purpose. The sloping floor is inclined towards the high altar for better viewing, and the rhythm of the pews is set out to accommodate the different states of minds of the various patients, with doors nearby so that people could be removed quickly if they weren't well. The confessionals are designed to be more open so that the patients can always be seen, and here the joinery is particularly well resolved.

We drew direct inspiration from this church when designing the interior of the Sans Souci hotel in Vienna recently. We were able to use the same hanging lights in the café and also borrowed the idea of the fluted walls and stone datum for the restaurant. Our lobby floor has a decorative marble inlay and we've used plenty of gold tracery in the bedrooms.

Whereas in London often we find new uses for nineteenth- and twentieth-century civic buildings, here this building is still publicly accessible and in use more than 100 years later as part of the hospital. In the context of our culture of PFI healthcare, it's amazing to find such an artistically important collection of buildings still in their original use.

While the building has many qualities, it is perhaps most notable for its ability to link the smallest decorative details, such as the infinitely reflecting engraved glass in the altar, back to address the church and the landscape and city beyond.

This creates a building linking heaven and earth that can be said to be genuinely contemplative. And while it is set within an architectural tradition that reaches back to the seventeenth-century churches of Brunelleschi and Borromini, this is very much a modern building.

Above: The church interior is overwhelmingly white with light gold tracery and modern abstract decoration.

Opposite: The church's gold dome and hilltop position made it a landmark over all Vienna. It is still in use as a hospital church.

VIENNESE WHIRL Leading Viennese architect Otto Wagner (1841–1918) provoked controversy with his design of a spectacular Catholic church at the Steinhof asylum for the mentally ill on the outskirts of the city. Though now revered as the first modern church in Europe and a fine example of ecclesiastical Jugendstil, the church was widely criticised on its completion for being too austere and stylised in its decoration when expectations were for a more baroque style.

The negative reaction effectively ended Wagner's career. Wagner masterplanned the 144-ha asylum grounds as a series of pavilions within a landscape, with the church at the top of the site reached by a broad flight of steps.

Care was taken to accommodate the needs of the congregation. The church is north-south facing to give less harsh indirect light. Extra side doors allow for swift exits for those unable to settle. Restored in 2006, the church is still used by hospital residents.

Michael Squire enjoys the "single palette of infinite brick" at Grundtvig's Church in Copenhagen.

Grundtvig's Church

Location: Copenhagen, Denmark

Architect: Peder Vilhelm Jensen-Klint

Completed: 1913–40

Chosen by Michael Squire of Squire and Partners

In Denmark, brick is an ordinary material. But at Grundtvig's Church, the architect Peder Vilhelm Jensen-Klint makes it extraordinary. I first visited a few years ago on an office trip to Copenhagen, and as I engaged with the building I found it increasingly compelling. It demonstrates how a building can be a contemporary image of its time while remaining grounded in its culture.

The exterior of the church is powerful and expressive – with roots in gothic, classical and local Danish architecture. Its shapes are drawn from organic crystalline forms and contemporary futurist images, but they are organised within the framework of a traditional Zealand village church.

Having viewed the exterior of the building, I didn't really know what to expect of the inside – it could have been an over-scaled timber barn. Instead there was this poetic array of soaring vaults made from the same buttery brick used on the outside, but here they were polished and their colour preserved. The effect is calm and restrained, yet enormously powerful.

So many things are at play in this church but Jensen-Klint expresses them economically through the use of a single element manipulated in numerous different ways. In doing so, he turns everything that is gothic – except the structure – on its head and creates something poetic out of such a basic material. In this way, there is a link to NFS Grundtvig himself – who the church was built as a monument to – because he, too, celebrated the simplicity and ordinariness of traditional Danish culture, and believed education based on this simplicity would enrich rather than debase Danish cultural life.

The appeal of this building is how it is rooted in the history and culture of the place in which it is built – its *genius loci*. I love how Jensen-Klint referred to the church as built culture. Yet it remains a completely contemporary work. My own architectural aspirations stem from the notion that a building should be culturally connected to where it is.

Jensen-Klint loved the vernacular of village churches and his design for Grundtvig's Church comes from this very simple pastoral Protestant tradition rather than a smells-and-bells Catholicism. As a result, it is very much part of where it is in Denmark – you really couldn't drop it down anywhere else.

Jensen-Klint was an engineer before he became an architect, and thought architects should be trained to build rather than design. He was extraordinarily hands-on, visiting the site every day for 12 years and drawing every detail necessary for the construction. I admire how he pursued his dream relentlessly from winning the competition in 1913 to finding a site, fundraising, and then drawing every aspect of the design for over a decade. Although he died 10 years before the building was finished, he had the satisfaction of knowing that his design was complete. He'd left nothing to chance.

The site found for Jensen-Klint's competition-winning design was to be at the heart of a new housing development. Although classical plans were proposed for the housing layout by Copenhagen city planners, Jensen-Klint adapted these to a freer, more medieval layout.

The original plans proposed positioning the tallest residential buildings closer to the church, stepping up in scale towards it, but Jensen-Klint typically wanted the opposite. The result is that the church rises dramatically with far greater contrast to the surrounding housing.

The housing was eventually almost entirely taken over and detailed by Jensen-Klint. The architectural language drew upon the arts and crafts movement, but understanding the cost and consequent elitism that led to its demise, Jensen-Klint kept the housing extremely simple and affordable with the exception of the articulated doorways that brought a uniqueness to each group of dwellings.

The interior has been criticised for being a pastiche and the vaults are certainly rooted in the gothic tradition, but there isn't a single piece of decoration – no stained glass, art or even crosses – and no sense of the church trying to control the congregation through such things.

There is no storytelling here, and no tricks. Instead, there is a single palette of infinite brick that just expresses structure. There is a tremendous variety in the shades of the brick – some pink, some orange, some yellow – but, like tweed, they all read as one.

This one brick module is used in an amazing array of ways – in a herringbone pattern on the floor; slightly canted for the arches; turned on its side as a sailor course to give the suggestion of a capital at the springing of the arches; and pushed inwards into the entrance lobby to give depth to the three doorways on the outside, which makes reference to cathedrals such as Notre Dame or Chartres.

Just as Louis Kahn talked about respecting brick, here it is celebrated, and is absolutely true to the building. It just does what it is supposed to do and you see every piece of the

construction. The church was criticised when first completed on the grounds that it was inappropriate as a monument to Grundtvig and for its remodelling of the humble Protestant church-hall tradition, but I think this use of brick brings it right back down to earth.

Architects were seduced in the twentieth century by the notion of manufactured buildings, but this church is the result of crafted engineering rather than a factory product. It is reported that only nine bricklayers were used throughout the entire construction period to lay five million bricks, working at a rate of 150 bricks per day, rather than the usual rate of 1,500 or so.

You can see the skill everywhere, particularly in the way the courses of brick are stitched together in the vaults of the crypt. Nothing is wilful. It's all beautifully logical. Every brick that went into the interior was polished before it was put into place. This was madness, but a beautiful madness and demonstrates a truly monumental rigour.

Grundtvig's Church has had the problem of being an ecclesiastical building in a materialist age. But this building possesses such spirituality and timelessness that I'm sure it will be cherished for centuries to come.

The dramatic front elevation of the memorial Grundtvig's Church, which sat at the heart of a new housing development on the edge of the city.

MONUMENT IN BRICK Grundtvig's Church is a memorial to NFS Grundtvig (1783–1872), a priest, hymn writer and educator credited with a pivotal role in forming modern Danish national consciousness.

A competition for a memorial to him was won in 1913 by the architect Peder Vilhelm Jensen-Klint (1853-1930), who proposed building a church. His vision was for a dramatically scaled-up version of a Danish village church based on those in medieval rural Zealand, but with decidedly gothic influences. He was also strongly influenced by the architects Peter Behrens and Fritz Höger (see pp14–19) from Germany, who were also using brickwork imaginatively at the time. Using bricks delivered in straw from Zealand, the building programme began in 1921 and the tower was inaugurated in 1927.

After Jensen-Klint died in 1930, his son, Kaare Klint, took over, completing the adjacent housing development in 1936 and building the rest of the church to his father's designs. In total, almost five million bricks were used throughout the 1,440-seater church.

Like the rest of the church, the crypt is made entirely of brick with the only decoration derived from variation in the brick courses.

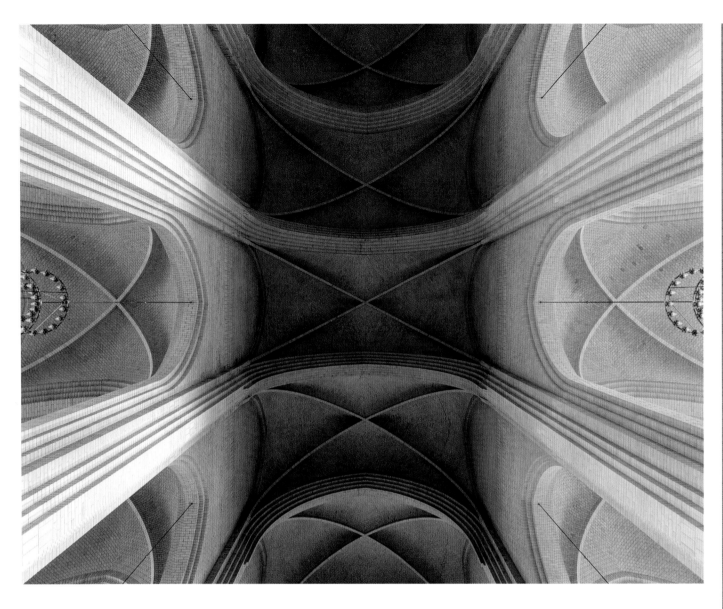

Above: Soaring brick vaults. The church's design draws on gothic, classical and local Danish vernacular influences.

Right: View towards the altar. Michael Squire admires the "truly monumental rigour" of the brick-led design.

Ted Cullinan in the main
chapel of Notre Dame Du
Haut at Ronchamp, which
he first visited when it was
newly completed in 1955.

Chapel of Notre Dame Du Haut

Location: Ronchamp, France
Architect: Le Corbusier
Completed: 1950–55
Chosen by Ted Cullinan of Cullinan Studio

It's four o'clock in the afternoon, the end of a lovely October day. I'm sitting on the stone pyramid at Ronchamp, built to commemorate the countless Maquis partisans and paratroopers who died recapturing this southern outcrop of the Vosges mountains in eastern France.

In front of me is the east front of Le Corbusier's chapel, which replaced a previous chapel destroyed in the Second World War. To my left is the grass roof of Corb's unbelievably sophisticated yet naïve Hotel des Pelerins, which visually supports and finishes the edge of the small smooth grass plateau on which the chapel of Notre Dame du Haut, the pyramid, and a set of bells, all sit. Around the other edges of this plateau are trees with a few gaps in them that allow views of rolling hills to the south, and the Vosges to the north and the east.

This is exactly where I sat in October 1955, aged 24, after I had cycled from London along wet pavé, through dirty villages and some dungy countryside with big splashy camions going by closely, and DS19s (for car buffs) going by fast and futuristically. I was dressed in flappy khaki shorts and an ex-army top. I was exhausted, sweaty and filthy of course, having pushed my bike up the kilometre track that led from Ronchamp's (then) village to the chapel at the top of the hill. But I was also elated by my walk around the outside of Corb's masterwork and my exploration of the unbelievably moving interior. And I was a Catholic in those days! So I might have been a bit stoned then by this combination of circumstances.

Today's repeat sit, so many years later, is a good test and here is the answer to that test. Yes, Le Corbusier's chapel is still the most profoundly moving and consummate work of architectural art of the 20th century – a century that includes Picasso, Stravinsky and so many others to love.

So here I am again at the eastern end of the chapel, the backdrop to outside masses on feast days. This is in full shadow, but the composition of altar, cross, pulpit and revolving Virgin and child (who else could possibly pull that off?), all together under the giant porch formed by the dipping concrete roof, is so perfect that even in shadow it contributes greatly to this utterly lovely, historically profound hilltop.

The deep and calming joy I feel as I sit here is so fulfilling that it supersedes the many jarring notes that accompanied my approach to the chapel on this revisit.

To get to Saint Notre Dame du Haut, you now travel up a neat paved road that rises and falls and gently curves up along the line of the historic dirt track I walked up in 1955, till you abruptly arrive at a white concrete car park, which here crosses at right angles Corb's original Ronchamp approach path, shut off now by a belligerent, sliding galvanised gate.

Straight ahead is the whitish concrete path to the new visitor centre so that you have to pay up before being allowed to the other side of a crass concrete wall and back onto the master's approach path. In the distance, above all this jagged whitish concrete, Le Corbusier's chapel sits powerful and serene in its perfectly well-balanced way, of raw concrete and white-painted sprayed-on render. So what can all these white walls and roads do but look utterly jagged and trivial with the chapel so close?

Now let me say that the new convent building by Renzo Piano Building Workshop is most beautifully detailed. And its position around the corner and further down the hill than in Piano's first proposal is surely not bad where it is. But the visitor centre, similarly but slightly less subtly composed, is, in as much as it is part of the jagged entrance to the site, much less satisfactory. But why are they both here? Surely a simple cable railway could bring you up through the woods from a car park and visitor centre in Ronchamp and drop you on Le Corbusier's diagonal approach, while the top third of the present roadway could be grassed over to make a lovely walk up. Then the convent containing the delightful and very helpful sisters could stay or not. Maybe our gentler descendants might consider some such solution.

Having negotiated the obstacle course required by mammon, one finds oneself back on Corb's approach path. On my return visit the chapel interior is as moving as ever – a wondrously calm place within white walls beneath the great curved sagging concrete roof and lit four ways: by a crack where the walls arrive at the roof; by the astonishing varied light entering through the south wall; by the light that descends down the three towers; and by other cracks and dots in the west wall.

There are no windows, just various light sources making atmosphere.

But I do have some quibbles. If the three top-lit side chapels are ever to be as sublime again as they originally were, the glass needs cleaning at the top of the three towers and the now grubby interior walls need painting white again. Also, the choir should again sing from the inside/outside balcony Corb provided instead of huddled along a wall on naff bits of temporary furniture as they did at the mass I attended. And

the priest or others should preach from the original pulpit rather than from a temporary one erected for each service. They might also tone down the excessive floodlighting of the chapel at night. Surely just the tower with a hint of something beside it would do. And then we might recover the whole of this little paradise in the Vosges.

Fifty-seven years ago I cycled home by a longer route to get a feel for the Vosges and I encountered a dusting of snow. Today, I came and will go by TGV and it's a blissfully sunny Indian summer morning. But Ronchamp is just the same.

VIRTUOSO CHAPEL Commissioned by the Roman Catholic Church, Le Corbusier's Pilgrimage Chapel of Notre Dame du Haut at Ronchamp marked a radical departure in his oeuvre.

The chapel responded to the hilltop site with its dramatic views of the Vosges mountains. Its distinctive oversailing concrete roof is supported on thick columns embedded within the thick walls. The interior is dominated by the drama of the south wall, with its mass of windows filled with different coloured glass. As well as the main chapel, Ronchamp contains three smaller, top-lit chapels including the red chapel, named after the intense colour of its walls.

When completed in 1955, the chapel confused and shocked the architectural great and good. More than half a century later, there was fresh controversy when a new visitor centre and a convent – designed by Renzo Piano Building Workshop – was widely criticised for compromising the original approach route to the chapel.

Above: Stained-glass windows set in a deep niche in the south wall of the main chapel.

Opposite: South-east view, with the outdoor pulpit, cross and altar visible to the right and the dramatic south wall to the left.

Above: Enamelled panels designed by Le Corbusier at the entrance to the chapel.

View towards the altar in
the main chapel. The south
wall admits light through
27 deep-set windows.

North-east view of the
chapel, which is positioned
on a hilltop with extensive
views of the countryside.

Above: St Peter's Church in Klippan. Visiting it was a "mind-blowing" experience for architect Patrick Lynch.

Opposite: The altar, like the rest of the church, is clad in uncut bricks.

St Peter's Church

Location: Klippan, Sweden
Architect: Sigurd Lewerentz.
Completed: 1962–66
Chosen by Patrick Lynch of Lynch Architects

Lewerentz has been called a 'silent architect', but for me his architecture is completely the opposite. Witty, humorous and never boring, it speaks absolutely eloquently.

Until I visited St Peter's I'd only seen it in dark, gloomy photographs. But when I saw it for myself it was mind-blowingly amazing and wonderful – a physical, visceral and intellectual shock. It's one of my top three buildings ever, and became the key to my PhD on the communicative movement between site, architecture and sculpture.

Because it's so dark inside it takes a while for your eyes to adjust. Then you realise how Lewerentz has very, very cleverly orchestrated a stage set awaiting the action of worship. People say there's no iconography here but there is. It's just that the images are spatial and have become part of the architecture.

Lewerentz was deeply religious and had an expert client in the theologian Lars Ridderstedt, who had the provocative idea of naming the church St Peter – ie the rock – an illusion to the place name of Klippan which means cliff or rock in Swedish. What Lewerentz did that was so brilliant was to retrospectively embed the place in time, effectively creating a new foundation myth for a town named after a rock by making a connection between the river at Klippan and the River Jordan.

In Sweden, the importance of processions and saints' festivals survived within Lutheranism. Services celebrate a condensed form of the traditional Way of the Cross pilgrimage through the breaking of bread and by depicting some sort of physical movement towards something before coming back. At St Peter's, there is a very clear direction of movement through the space. This is a very powerful experience. You begin in the vestibule which is also the marriage chapel, where Lewerentz placed a model boat in reference to St Peter's life as a fisherman in front of the brick waves of the vaults. Entering the main church, worshippers move past an extraordinary font before taking their seats. Here, Lewerentz takes the symbol of the conch shell that in traditional paintings John the Baptist used to baptise Jesus, and positions it overflowing with water from a cistern. It drips, every second, down into a deep channel below.

You don't see the cross at first. Formed by a Corten steel structural column and beam, it becomes most apparent as a cross on a hill when seen from a child's height from the entrance at the east. When you go towards the altar to take communion you walk under a huge hanging blue tapestry designed by Sven Erixson. But when you turn back, it appears red from the other side – symbolising the Passion and the redeeming blood of Christ – and the vaults appear before you like brick clouds.

When the west gate is opened in summer the congregation looks out towards the lake and can see heaven reflected on the water in the form of the clouds in the sky. After processing out of the church, they pass three angled lampposts, which quite clearly represent Christ and the two thieves on the cross. St Peter's is a whole landscape of images that spatialise those events in the Holy Land that make up Christian belief and form the basis of the Eucharistic service. While there are no icons or paintings, it's a sort of built Sunday School lesson.

To understand St Peter's you really need to go there and experience it as part of the congregation. It only really makes sense in use. Otherwise, you're missing the point.

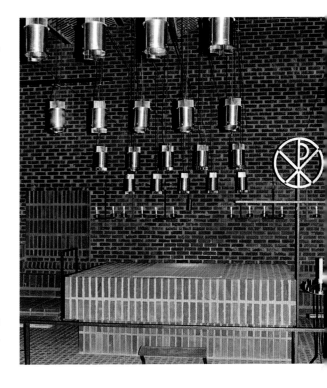

SPATIAL ICONOGRAPHY St Peter's Church and community centre was completed in 1966 at the former hamlet of Alby, which had grown since 1945 into a small town based on a nascent textile industry, and was renamed Klippan, which means cliff in Swedish, after a rock in the local river.

Built using uncut bricks, the design of the church is deliberately dark and primitive. The design was driven by the spatial needs of the liturgy and in particular by the progress of the worshipper through and out of the space during a service. Landscaped gardens with a shallow lake form an integral part of the scheme.

Paul Monaghan at the
Metropolitan Cathedral of
Christ the King, popularly
known as 'Paddy's Wigwam'.

Metropolitan Cathedral Of Christ The King

Location: Liverpool, UK

Architect: Frederick Gibberd

Completed: 1967

Chosen by Paul Monaghan of Allford Hall Monaghan Morris

This building was my first exposure to modern architecture. As a child I went to a Catholic school in Liverpool – St Edward's College – and every year we went to the Metropolitan Cathedral for St Edward's Day.

At the time the building was fascinating to me with its very strong form and, once inside, all that light and colour. Liverpool in the 1960s was very dirty and messy, still peppered with bomb sites, prefabs and black smog-stained buildings. And here was this beautiful building, seeming to emerge up out of the grime, so full of light, art and sculpture. It was part of the great period of post-war architecture in the fifties and sixties, a very optimistic period in Liverpool – the docks were still working, the Beatles were in their heyday – and this building captures something of that optimism.

It quickly became known as Paddy's Wigwam as people immediately adopted it as their own. I think this was one of the first times a building was given a popular nickname, and I liked the idea that a building could become an icon for the city. It was uncompromisingly modern, but at the same time very popular.

I have learnt many things from this building, but perhaps the most powerful lesson has been that modern buildings built with pride and integrity can be really loved by the public.

Aware that the Anglican Cathedral was being built in Liverpool at the same time, Frederick Gibberd changed his design so that the two buildings would complement each other on the city's skyline. He introduced the tall spires on the top to give a more vertical emphasis and make the proportions of his cathedral more slender. Although these may look like a crown on top of the building, for Gibberd they were

functional – the diagonals between the spires acting as cross-bracing against the wind.

I think this cathedral is a hidden gem although it is often referred to pejoratively when compared to Niemeyer's Metropolitan Cathedral in Brasilia. A lot of people think Gibberd copied Niemeyer, but in fact the Liverpool building was finished three years earlier.

As an architecture student, I began to learn about Gibberd's sources for the building, such as Le Corbusier's Ronchamp (see pp192–197) and particularly Basil Spence's Coventry Cathedral, where the structure and form are more elegantly integrated. But even as a child, I could see that it was very legible as a structure. It really is like a huge tent or wigwam with ring beams and ties that were structurally very cost-effective. The building had a budget of £1 million, which even then was remarkably cheap for a cathedral, and here was another lesson: the job of the architect is to make something special happen without the need for huge budgets.

The competition brief for the cathedral stipulated that everyone in the congregation should be as near to the altar as possible, and Gibberd concluded that to achieve this the worship needed to be in the round. This was quite radical for a Catholic cathedral at the time. Standing here, what strikes me most as I revisit the building is the quality of the light and the drama of the space. Then there are the colours, which are very beautiful especially the blue and red elements.

Most churches at the time were representational in their decoration but this was far more abstract. The baldacchino (suspended canopy) or 'crown of thorns' floating above

the altar is the key element of focus within the sacristy. As a functional architect, Gibberd didn't want anything in the building to be read as a metaphor, even though he realised that sometimes this was inevitable. In this case, the canopy carries the lighting rig and the speakers, so manages to be both functional and also symbolic.

The plans for this building are very elegant, with the arrangement of different-shaped chapels around the edge, each with their own character but at the same time connecting into the main space. The Lady Chapel is almost a church in itself.

While the powerful spatial elements dominate, it is the details and collaborations that make this building so special A large number of artists were commissioned to create works throughout the building and in particular, the peripheral chapels. These works complement and enhance the building overall. For example, the wall hangings in the main space have the dual purpose of helping the acoustics by counteracting the many hard surfaces.

Then there are the striking colours within the stained-glass tower designed by John Piper, who also created the windows for Coventry Cathedral. Interestingly, they were innovatively constructed using pre-cast panels which stand to this day despite some major refurbishment work.

Whenever I visit I always enjoy the great bell tower entrance at the cathedral and how it relates to Hope Street. To save money, the sliding doors were constructed from GRP and clad with a bronze overlay depicting the four apostles. Above are the bells Matthew, Mark, Luke and John.

There have been changes over the years. There was a lot of innovation in the original construction, some of which didn't work – the building certainly leaked. It had a big refurbishment in the nineties, including a rather crude reworking of the buttresses, which were originally covered with mosaic.

The acoustic atmosphere was such a big part of the experience of the building. It had notoriously slow acoustics – one note used to take five seconds to reverberate. When I had to give a speech there for a school prize-day service, I practised speaking really slowly, but I didn't need to – somehow they've corrected the sound digitally.

The new entrance steps, designed by my old school friend Paul Falconer of Falconer Chester Hall, work very well and give the cathedral a more civic feel at ground level. However, the rear of the cathedral with its outdoor chapel now feels a touch neglected. It's just too austere. Perhaps they should have a design competition for it – add a bit of twenty-first-century thinking to this piece of classic twentieth century modernist architecture.

Blessed Sacrament Chapel, one of many smaller chapels positioned around the perimeter to give more intimate spaces for worship.

The Baldacchino canopy sits below the stained-glass tower in the Cathedral's main space. The circular design ensured that all the congregation could be close to the altar.

CROWNING GLORY Frederick Gibberd's Metropolitan Cathedral was a cut-price replacement for a grandiose scheme by Edwin Lutyens, abandoned in the late fifties. In 1960 a design competition was launched with just a £1 million budget for the shell structure. Gibberd's circular design was chosen from 300 entries. It was consecrated in 1967, and holds a congregation of 2,300.

The Grade II* listed building is notable for Gibberd's collaboration with several artists, notably John Piper who, with Patrick Reyntiens, created the stained-glass window depicting the Blessed Trinity. Other artists include Elisabeth Frink, Ceri Richards and William Mitchell, who created the bronze sliding doors and the carvings on the Portland stone bell tower.

Unfortunately, the building soon began to suffer structural and leakage problems, and in the eighties the archdiocese launched a legal claim against the architect and the builder, eventually settling out of court. An £8 million refurbishment began in 1992, and in 2003 Gibberd's envisaged ceremonial steps were finally completed.

Public Buildings

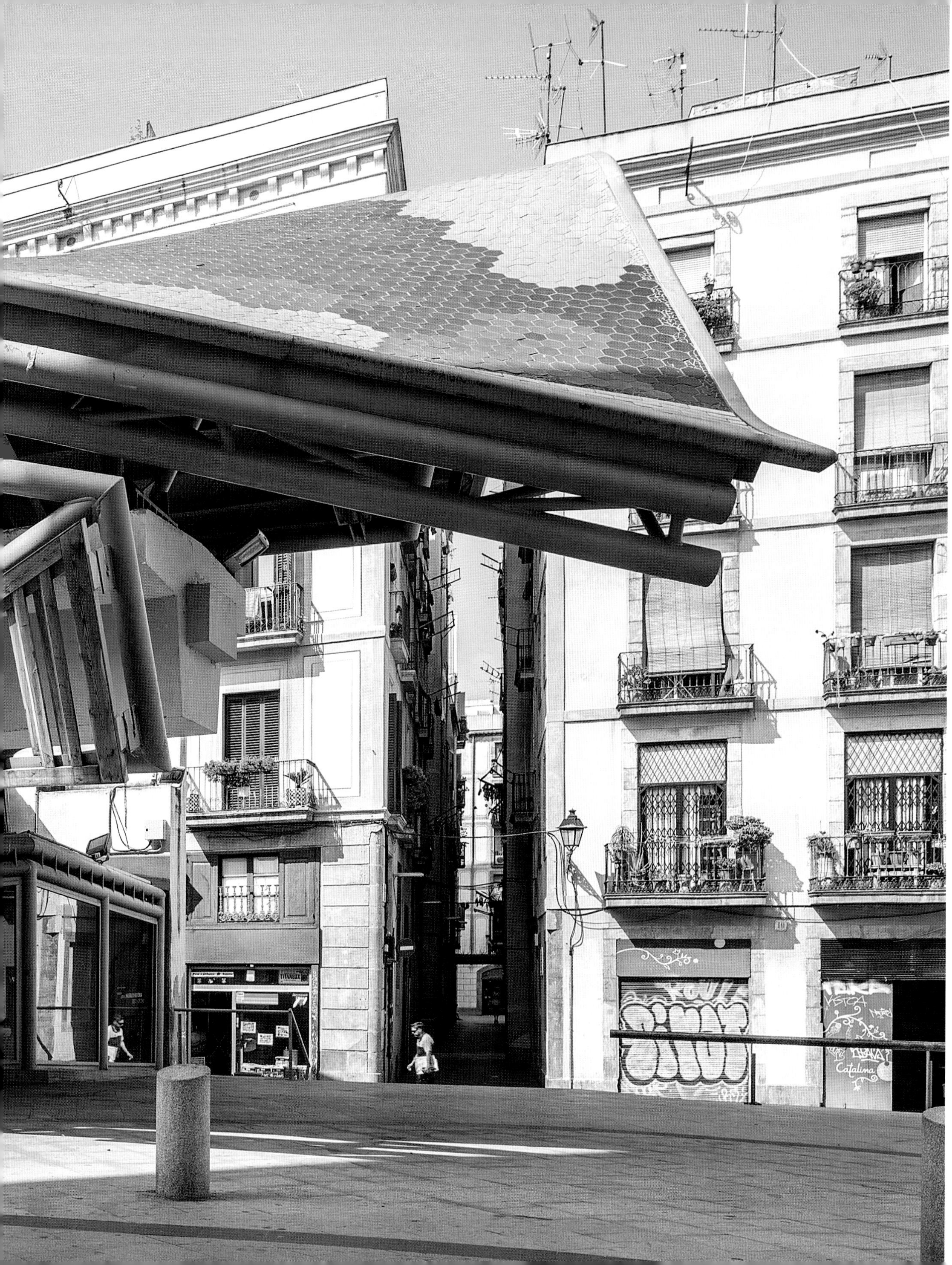

Lucy the Elephant, originally created to sell real estate, is admired by Tom Coward, for its "familiarity and otherness".

Lucy the Elephant

Location: Margate, New Jersey, USA
Developer/engineer: James V Lafferty
Architect: William Free
Completed: 1881
Chosen by Tom Coward of AOC

Lucy the Elephant is a remarkable technical achievement – both materially and structurally – and is especially important because of the journey she has been on within her community.

People often dumb down the eccentric side of Victorian culture which was as complicated and varied as our own in terms of taste. Lucy is an example of one of the extremes of that age.

A number of years after finding out about her, I found myself on the East Coast and went on a short pilgrimage to Lucy to see how she was.

Lucy was a spectacular concept by a property developer called James Lafferty. She's lasted more than 130 years. In that time her role has constantly shifted, and also the way something of such 'exotic' form could capture different imaginations at different times. Part of the reason it's lasted is that it's thought to be useful by lots of different people.

It's very specific, an elephant, but it's also flexible, and you can do whatever you like with it: its generous elephant nature has helped it do that. It got to the point where it meant enough to people in the town for them to save it.

The relationship between obvious metaphor and architecture is common but very few architects are willing to be honest that their work relies on it. But even if they don't notice the associations, the public will, as they have with the Gherkin. Lucy also possibly has as much of a relationship with pop art as she does with modern architecture.

Lafferty and his architect treated the elephant much like any building project, and I like the bravery of that. She was modelled by boat builders, a local craft, and her final form was an additive process.

The exterior is tin, which was a good material to curve around the complex geometry of the elephant's form. I don't know of many other examples of 120-year-old double curvature cladding systems.

She dominates the town. The only other big structure is the water tower, and that has a picture of Lucy on it. It's fascinating that something like her exists, popping up over standard lot houses in this quiet seaside town two miles south of Atlantic City.

Visitors approach her from behind and walk between her legs into a gathering space. She feeds from a bucket, so has five legs really. You go in through one leg and climb up a very tight spiral staircase into a triple-height main hall through the hip. It's like a boat, with a raised forecastle serving as a stage. At the front, you can go into closets which have porthole eyes. I like how you get a weird mix of elephant, paint graphics, boat structure interior, and standard domestic elements such as doors and windows. And there's a suggestive window inserted just below the tail!

The combination is very interesting, architecturally speaking. It's got a raw quality, it's certainly not hi-tech or precious. The important thing appears to be the play between familiarity and otherness, and that is something we attempt with our work.

Lucy is a relevant piece of architecture because she reminds me that traditions of architecture are not reductive, closed systems but subject to change, and that ideas like pop and spectacle are actually antique in our modern age.

The other highlight of my trip to see Lucy was Frank Lloyd Wright's Falling Water. Falling Water is a building full of love, care and ambition, but perhaps more surprisingly, so is an elephant.

ELEPHANT HOUSE Lucy the Elephant was built in 1881 by engineer and land speculator James Lafferty as a stunt to promote home sales near Atlantic City. Since then, she's served variously as a private house, hotel, tavern, café and museum.

Lucy is an example of the eccentric architecture of the late Victorian age. Standing six storeys (just under 20m) high, Lucy weighs in at around 82 tonnes and is covered in an estimated 1,115sq m of hammered sheet tin, supported on 8,560 arches or ribs. The legs contain the stairs and the body is divided into rooms, with more stairs leading to the howdah.

Lafferty secured a patent for constructing animal-shaped buildings in 1882. Lucy, who became a famous attraction, was the only one to survive, after a local rescue campaign moved her on wheels to a new site in 1970. She is the only elephant to be designated a US National Historic Landmark.

Sean Griffiths enjoys a
cocktail at the American
Bar in Vienna, a tiny bar
packed full of ideas at a
time when Europe was on
the cusp of great change.

American Bar

Location: Vienna, Austria
Architect: Adolf Loos
Completed: 1908
Chosen by Sean Griffiths

The American Bar is an astonishing interior. As well as being a very radical piece of early twentieth-century design, as Europe's first ever cocktail bar it brought a decadent New World experience to an old imperial Europe on the verge of catastrophic dissolution.

I was brought here the first time I came to Vienna in 1997 and it made a huge impression on me. What was immediately apparent was the way that Adolf Loos used mirrors so effectively, not only to create reflection and the illusion of rooms beyond the one you were in, but to place emphasis on the illusion of infinite space itself. I'm not aware of this having been done before, and as such it introduces the modern idea of 'space' as opposed to rooms. Yet it retains its quality as a discrete room.

One of the most resonant reasons for choosing this bar is its size. It's tiny. We live in a time when buildings are not considered important unless they're big. But this little bar has far more ideas packed into it than all those huge buildings put together.

I also like that it is a bar – the sort of thing architects might do at the start of their careers while thinking they'll move on to bigger and supposedly better things. The bar also unequivocally avoids the worthiness and moralising that forms one of the less attractive features of modernism.

Instead of being about social improvement — that sense of forcing the world to be a better place through architecture — it's about intimacy, sociability and conviviality. In contrast to whiter-than-white modernism, its whisky-hued interior has something both aristocratic and rather sleazy about it, undoubtedly reflecting the character of the man himself.

You can trace so many things that people have designed over the last 100 years back to this. There is much in this tiny space that reappears in twentieth-century art and architecture.

Its time and location are important. Paris is often thought of as the centre of European modernism, but in 1908, during the last years of the Habsburg Empire, Vienna was the cultural centre of the world. Architecturally, it was the home of the Vienna secessionist movement, a last bastion of imperialism that Loos himself was opposed to because of its use of decoration. At the same time Vienna was home to an array of innovators revolutionising convention across many different fields. These include Sigmund Freud, the inventor of psychoanalysis, Arnold Schoenberg, creator of the 12-tone system that dominated twentieth-century classical music, philosopher Ludwig Wittgenstein and the critical writer Karl Kraus. The latter three certainly knew Loos and you could create an enticing fiction that they would sit drinking together in this very spot.

Other connections abound. The bar has a distinctly surreal quality. It's big and small, rational and irrational, modernist and classical. The mirrors anticipate Freud's writing on narcissism, published in 1914, and yet the ego libido is denied, as the main mirror reflects not the person but the space, the idea of a space that is empty.

But as you sip a cocktail, and begin to melt into the environment, in the secondary mirrors placed between the columns below the heightened dado, through a dreamy haze of smoke and conversation, you capture a reflected image from your seat, a glimpse of the life of a tiny bar that is overflowing and far from empty. Only when you look from the back seat towards the door does the narcissistic moment recur, as you catch a glimpse of yourself, perhaps a little intoxicated and loose-tongued, in the mirror next to the door.

Freud was a key influence for the surrealists, many of whom Loos would also have known. But I wonder if Marcel Duchamp ever strayed into this place? Would he have admired the chequerboard floor, reminding him of his passion for chess? If you were to make his *Large Glass* (1915–23) as architecture, it might have looked like this. Would he have noted the sign at the front? This is a three-dimensionalised, tilted American flag made from fragments of glass – an objet trouvé made of objets trouvés and the first example I can think of where a sign is used so architecturally.

The glass fragments in the flag sign recall not only the *Large Glass* but also the encaustic flags of the painter Jasper Johns who later became a friend of Duchamp. So here we have conceptualism and pop art prefigured too.

The coppery eroticism of the *Large Glass* is also present in this interior, a notion which is highly suggestive of both Loos's and Duchamp's voyeurism. The result is not unequivocally modernist. But its stripped-back nature, the quality and use of materials anticipate modernism. In this bar, Loos is on the cusp of the shift from the vertical to the horizontal that characterised modernism but it still has the sense of a classical space with its hypostyle array of regular columns and reference to the Pantheon roof in its marble coffering. How much does Mies van der Rohe's Barcelona pavilion (see pp80–81) owe to this place, which he surely visited? How many buildings of any size have all these connections flowing backwards and forwards?

But, we shouldn't forget it is a bar, after all. There's something burlesque and music hall about it with all its mirrors, illuminated tables and sensuous materials. It has a touch of the transatlantic liner about it, with furniture built in to create little intimate spaces within spaces. But the mirrored lobby (including the ceiling) also makes you think of a Soho strip bar.

So, Loos had gone to America for a few years previously and had fallen in love with it. He was at the very cusp of the collapse of one European empire and the beginning of a new epoch in America. Bowled over by American culture, he came back to Vienna and created an American cocktail bar, complete with a stars and stripes flag projected over the door.

Revisiting the bar, I can see how important it is to get the feeling of the place by having a drink here and experiencing its dreamy atmosphere. It should be thought of as a total environment. What's in the glass is as important as the space itself.

View towards the entrance, with the bar to the right and the onyx-clad wall above. The coffered ceiling design references the Pantheon roof.

Above, left: Seating booth with mahogany panelling and mirrors that give the illusion of a far larger space. The table is internally illuminated.

Above, right: The exterior incorporates marble pillars and a 3D representation of an American flag. The bar was Europe's first cocktail bar.

SMOKE AND MIRRORS The Moravian-born architect Adolf Loos (1870-1933) designed this tiny cocktail bar in an existing building in the Kärntner Durchgang in central Vienna.

The bar, also known as the Kärntner Bar and latterly the Loos Bar, was one of his earlier works after his return from America, where he was influenced by Louis Sullivan's buildings in Chicago. At the time, Loos was vocally opposed to the Vienna secession movement, denouncing ornamentation as crime. His later work included the Steiner House (1910) and Michaelerplatz House (1911) in Vienna, and Villa Müller (1928) in Prague. On the exterior, the frontage has four rectangular Skyros marble piers with a projected sign above created in tesserae. Customers enter the tiny space through a heavy leather curtain off a tiny mirrored lobby.

Measuring just 5m long, 3.5m wide and 3.5m tall, it is clad in onyx and marble, with mahogany panelling and expanses of mirror on three sides that give the illusion of a much larger space. The bar runs the length of one side with two areas of leather banquette seating on either side of steep stairs to the basement.

Tony Fretton at Stockholm
Woodland Cemetery,
where the landscape and
buildings are imbued with
powerful symbolism.

Stockholm Woodland Cemetery

Location: Enskede, Sweden

Architects: Erik Gunnar Asplund and Sigurd Lewerentz

Completed: 1915–40

Chosen by Tony Fretton

I first saw the Woodland Cemetery about 15 years ago when I came to lecture in Stockholm one winter and the beauty of its composition was all the more evident in the snow. There is something very calming about this big landscape. Daily life rarely offers such moments. Everywhere you look there are lovely incidents that cohere empirically into a whole.

The force of the cemetery is in the landscaping, which was the formative idea in the competition that Asplund and Lewerentz won when they were young. Asplund worked on the cemetery for 25 years, his style changing as he explored modernism. Lewerentz was asked to leave the project and went on to design extraordinary buildings such as the church at Klippan (see pp 198–199). The competition-winning design was made in 1914, at the same time as highly abstract buildings were issuing from the modern movement in France and Germany. In comparison, Asplund and Lewerentz's reworking of traditional elements and their embrace of sentiment was old-fashioned.

But there were more routes to modernism than the modern movement. Karl Friedrich Schinkel found a vocabulary in classicism with which to address the functional and social issues of modern industrialising society and to some extent Asplund and Lewerentz did the same.

In the Woodland Cemetery, the issue was what to do with the dead of a growing urban population, functionally and meaningfully. Cremation, in which Lewerentz seems to have been an expert, was an answer. The landscaping, which is principally by Lewerentz, is the main means of resolving the functional and representational issues of this new way of interment. It conceals the crematorium by placing it underground, and provides significant settings for the chapels above.

The symbolism of the landscape is affecting and powerful but not through an appeal to any one faith. Sweden had already begun to acknowledge the diversity of faiths and beliefs of its population. In some way it is almost pagan, for example in the shallow pond and outdoor catafalque surrounded by blazing braziers in front of the Chapel of the Holy Cross, and the crooked trees on the top of the hill behind them.

In the buildings and landscape there is a very real sense of birth and rebirth, through subtle references to literature and buildings from antiquity. This is announced at the entrance to the cemetery by the striking asymmetric composition of the hill to one side and graveyards and chapels to the other, leading to the portico of the Chapel of the Holy Cross. The scale of this chapel allows for state funerals, its window-wall able to be lowered into the ground, allowing space for a very large group under the portico.

In contrast, the Woodland Chapel further on is a place for a discreet ceremony of a few people in the forest, while the Resurrection Chapel provides a dignified and plain classical setting.

Asplund's work was not in the foreground when I was studying at the Architectural Association. Instead I was looking at architects like Cedric Price and Hannes Meyer, where use and form closely coincide. I admired their view that modern buildings should be free of conventional meaning and simply provide conditions for sociability and interpretation by their users. I was also very interested in adaptable building forms that occupants could use obliviously, even crudely and destructively.

At the same time, I was affected by Alan Colquhoun's essay in Charles Jencks and George Baird's book *Meaning in Architecture*. This described Le Corbusier and Iannis Xenakis's attempt to strictly derive the form of the Philips Pavilion from its functions, and their discovery that it was impossible and choices had to be made using intuition and precedent. The full reconciliation of these ideas occurred when I was designing the Lisson Gallery and understood, through minimal and conceptual art, how meaning and use could coexist.

Making architecture purely for formal reasons seemed unreasonable to me and still does. But I had not reckoned on the impact of a younger generation, in the form of Mark Pimlott and Peter St John who at the time were working together and for a short time worked for me.

Le Corbusier, who was not formative to my generation as he was to the preceding one, was seen by them as a master of forms and ideas. The Smithsons, who were heroic practitioners to my generation, were gurus to theirs. And Asplund, who was a source of wonder to them, seemed from my hard-line position like a decorateur. Lewerentz was much more credible and affecting to me for his acute and existential understanding of materiality.

Although I admire Asplund's architecture very much, I cannot say that it influenced me. The interplay of modernity and tradition that I see in his work came to me much more strongly through Stravinsky, Joyce and Picasso. However Asplund was extremely skilled in understanding human experience and providing for it in his architecture. It is here, if anywhere, that I can relate to this work.

Whenever I am in Stockholm, I revisit the cemetery. You have to see it many times and in different seasons to be able to understand its different aspects.

SYMBOLIC LANDSCAPE Erik Gunnar Asplund and Sigurd Lewerentz won joint first prize in 1915 in the competition for a new cemetery for Stockholm. Asplund worked on the project for 25 years until his death in 1940. Lewerentz was involved until his removal from the project following the completion of his Resurrection Chapel in 1925.

The cemetery was created on 100ha of former quarry, transformed into a carefully created landscape of pine forests, grassy mounds, graves and chapels. Visitors enter and progress up to the imposing loggia of the crematorium and beyond to the Groves of Remembrance pine forest.

Asplund's first building on the site was the modest Woodland Chapel, 1918–20, which combined classicism with Swedish vernacular. Asplund completed the Woodland Crematorium and its Faith, Hope and Holy Cross chapels from 1935-40, each with their own antechamber and courtyard gardens for privacy and quiet contemplation. Along with Lewerentz's austere Resurrection Chapel, these offer a choice of type and size of funeral locations.

Above: A series of chapels lead to a grand portico for large gatherings with the Groves of Remembrance beyond.

Opposite: Graves line the procession from entrance to chapels. The crematorium is concealed by placing it underground.

Above: Chapel of
Resurrection, designed
by Sigurd Lewerentz and
completed in 1925.

Right: Woodland Chapel,
designed by Erik Gunnar
Asplund. Inaugurated in
1920, it is the cemetery's
smallest chapel.

MJ Long returns to
Zonnestraal Sanatorium,
which she first visited more
than 50 years ago when
much of it lay derelict.

Zonnestraal Sanatorium

Location: Hilversum, Netherlands
Architects: Jan Duiker with Bernard Bijvoet
Completed: 1926–31
Chosen by MJ Long of Long & Kentish

I first visited Zonnestraal in 1964, stumbling across it almost by accident when I was travelling around Europe. It was a revelation – touchingly naive and simple, and so unlike American corporate modernism, which was full of air-conditioning and suspended ceilings. As someone growing up in America, I hadn't seen modern architecture that was so cool, bare and modest, so minimal, so transparent… and so clearly related to a social programme and an idea about its relationship to popular culture.

Along with Jan Duiker's Handelsblad Cinema in Amsterdam and the Van Nelle Factory in Rotterdam, Zonnestraal was built at the moment when early modern Dutch architecture was at newest and most idealistic.

The client, the General Union of Dutch Diamond Workers, was interested in building a brave new world with a sanatorium that was modern and very much their own. And with Duiker they got their wish.

This was not a loose-fit building. Everything is almost quivering because it's so closely packed and tightly controlled.

It was designed around a very specific brief: to serve the needs of recovering tuberculosis patients in the period before antibiotics were developed. Duiker saw this as a specific task with a limited life; he therefore designed as a functionalist, happy the building would outlive its usefulness, rather than looking for the flexibility of a 'rational' architecture.

This is why it was so badly mauled when it was changed into a general hospital later on. The building is all about vertical and horizontal separation of circulation for inmates, visitors, incoming food, outgoing waste, locations for showers and laundries. In its consideration of cross-contamination, it is as complex and clear as a diagram for a law court.

The main building with communal facilities was built first, then the two ward pavilions, where you could easily wheel patients out to the terrace with the curtains forming a kind of sunshade over the bed. The two wings splay out to get the morning and afternoon light.

With the structural engineer Jan Gerko Wiebenga, Duiker and Bernard Bijvoet pushed the limits of structural minimalism, tightening up and paring away every bit of concrete they could until there was nothing left that could go. It's an incredible editing job and the result is taut and brave.

Duiker was trying to save money and to do the most with the least to create a language of architecture for the people. Although the frame is concrete, the walls are plaster on a wire mesh with an outer layer of white cement and were not originally painted.

The wards are based on a 3 metre structural module. This was because Dutch construction regulations meant you could strike formwork after only one week if the structural slab spanned no more than 3m. Otherwise you had to wait four weeks, which made a huge difference to the schedule. The resulting 3m cubes became the living unit for the individual, reproduced later in Bijvoet's captivating individual woodland huts with their awning windows and rotating bases to follow the sun like a flower.

All of the original buildings – the main building and the two residential ones that followed shortly after – are as simple as they can be in component and detail, but share a real architectural richness because of the care with which internal and external vistas have been composed. This is an ever-changing composition of offset hallways, compound vistas of inside and outside, with circular accents giving the whole a rich sculptural presence.

When I saw Zonnestraal in the 1960s it was in a poor state of repair, and had been extensively modified. The Dutch health authority would probably have been happy to pull it down and start anew, but the brave decision was taken to restore it to something as close to its original physical state as possible.

This made no economic sense. It would cost a great deal more than building a new building, and when finished would be difficult to find tenants for its very specific spaces. But it was thought to be so unique that it was worth spending the money.

The restoration was a tough job and Bierman Henket and Wessel de Jonge did it with great care. For every detail, the architects had to make a decision about whether to restore to the original condition or to the original principles of building. For instance, Duiker went for 25mm steel window sections in the main building, but five years later when he built the Dresselhuys Pavilion, he designed with 40mm steel window sections. The restoration architects felt that gave them permission to increase the cross-sections in the main building to about 30mm to allow them to get in double glazing where required. They also put in thin strips of high-spec insulation behind the plaster to reduce cold-bridging, introduced condensation drainage routes in the sill details, and raised the floor level to insert underfloor heating.

Originally the building used drawn glass for its glazing. Today's float glass would probably have appealed to Duiker because of its additional clarity, but drawn glass was considered more representative of the original look.

Henket and de Jonge found, of course, that few of the original mass-produced components were still available. Window handles were copied, and the look of the original steam pipes was preserved although they are not a very efficient part of the water-based heating system for the complex.

Returning to Zonnestraal after so long, I was interested to see whether the magic had gone after the restoration. There had been something touching about seeing it in a state of dereliction, and the tragedy of the ruin has now

gone. While it does feel almost too pristine, the freshness and lightness are still very moving.

What has been preserved is that moment when architecture was an idealistic part of a social programme, not a statement about style. This building keeps that idea alive. In 1964, I wouldn't have predicted this building would still be here and in use more than 50 years later – but it is, and I'm very glad to see it again.

The main sanatorium buildings. Although simple in component and detail, the building paid great attention to internal and external vistas and maximised views of the landscape.

HEALING ARCHITECTURE Zonnestraal was built between 1928 and 1931 as a rehabilitation centre for TB patients, designed by architects Jan Duiker (1890–1935) and Bernard Bijvoet (1889–1979) with structural engineer Jan Gerko Wiebenga (1886–1974).

It was organised around a central administration and communal facilities block, flanked by two pavilions of linear wards. There is also a 12-sided servants' accommodation building plus workshops and cabins. Patients were encouraged to work, making baskets while still bedridden, then spending time in the workshops, carrying out maintenance, as part of their rehabilitation.

As anticipated, new cures made the building redundant within a few decades and in 1957 the buildings became a general hospital, before falling into disrepair. Restoration of the main building took place from 2001 to 2003. The complex is now a multi-purpose health centre, while the servants' accommodation houses offices for a historic buildings lettings agency. Zonnestraal was nominated for the UNESCO World Heritage List in 1995.

A tightly proportioned staircase leads down from the roof terrace in the restored main building. Some parts of the sanatorium complex are still awaiting regeneration and new use.

Gothenburg Law Courts

Location: Gothenburg, Sweden
Architect: Erik Gunnar Asplund
Completed: 1937
Chosen by Tim Ronalds of Tim Ronalds Architects

Tim Ronalds admires the serenity and warmth of the extension to the Gothenburg Law Courts, a frequent source of inspiration.

There is something about Asplund's Law Courts at Gothenburg that confirms that being an architect is really worth the effort. Modern buildings so often seem quite shallow in their thinking. But then you see something like this and are reminded of what architecture at the very highest level can achieve.

Asplund was involved with the project for 24 years. Through the sequence of designs, you can trace his journey from national romanticism to classicism and then right at the end, just in time, this flowering of modernism.

There is an amazing difference between his 1925 design and the built scheme – you would think the time gap was a century, not a decade. Asplund was still changing the design of the front elevation as it was being built. My colleagues say that is really why I like Asplund so much – I too keep wanting to make late changes to our buildings.

Asplund must have been talked of when I was a student at Cambridge. However I was not impressed by the gloomy black-and-white photos of his buildings and it was a revelation when, in 1988, I saw Martin Charles's colour photos illustrating a marvellous essay on Asplund by Peter Blundell Jones. Instead of black-and-white Nordicism, these were full of sun and life. At the time, all was po-mo and almost everyone was stuttering backwards towards conservative and authoritarian attitudes. Here in Asplund was an example of what modern architecture could do to contribute to a humane and optimistic society.

The building has stood up incredibly well over the decades. I chose it not just because it is beautiful inside, but because of the spirit it embodies and the contrast it makes between

the modern and the classical, the twentieth century and the nineteenth. The old law court is a classical building with columns and pediments. It expresses the power of the law and visitors feel they shrink in size as they enter. Then they turn right to enter the extension and they find quite a different kind of architecture that sets the scene for humane justice.

In the old building you feel that you might get 'sent down'; in the new, that you will get a fair trial. It is dignified, but not intended to intimidate. It represented the new spirit of its time, not just in architecture but in society as a whole.

Asplund designed every element of the building – the furniture, the beautiful lights, the transparent sinks. It is very rare for an architect to have that much control of a design (or the talent to be able to do that); for a building to be a complete and consistent entity.

The outside of the Law Courts extension isn't the best bit and certainly doesn't convey the great quality of the interior. I enjoy the procession through the extension up the long, gentle staircase which takes you up in a calm and dignified way to the courtrooms on the first floor. Imagine the atmosphere in a courthouse – everyone's nerves on edge, the defendants, their families, the witnesses, the lawyers – but when they come in they find the warmth from the wood and all this light streaming in through the roof lights and through the glazed façade to the internal courtyard that separates the old and new buildings.

Inside, there are festive elements that simply lift the spirits. There is a wonderful dog-leg stair which feels a bit like a diving board and its finish seems to flow down like a pool of liquid

at the bottom. Attached to it is a clock looking like a sun with tiny light bulbs around its edge. Asplund loved curved and non-orthogonal forms in architecture, and was always trying to take the hard edges out of buildings.

The courtrooms themselves are womb-like with their curved wooden walls creating a scene for the theatre of a trial. The defendants sat with their backs to the public in front of the lay assessors and the judge, whose chair is distinguished only by its leather back. The lights in the courtrooms are fantastic – almost like Venus flytraps about to snap shut. The atmosphere is so different from that of traditional English courts with their crests and symbols of the state.

Asplund is one of the architects whose work I look at repeatedly for inspiration; not so much to copy ideas or forms directly, rather to recharge my aspirations. That said, I am surprised, coming back here, to realise how some of the elements of our music building for the University of Kent obviously have their origin in Gothenburg. The long louvred rooflight and sun falling on timber-panelled-walls – these images stick in the mind and resurface years later.

I know little about Asplund as a man, but his way of working seems inspiring. He was immensely inventive and had the capacity to reflect on the way life operates through design. Every aspect of the building has been studied creatively and thought through with originality. What distinguishes him from others is that he approached things from such a human point of view, making architecture that sets the scene for human theatre.

We spend a lot of time thinking about how people move through and experience buildings – more about what they feel like than what they look like. The Gothenburg building has a serenity about it that appeals to me. Through the use of wood, the building has a lot of warmth, and that is something I find myself endlessly thinking about in my work. Like Asplund, we take time to work at an idea – at Hackney Empire, there were some 40 different versions of that new elevation before the idea of the giant letters emerged.

Walking around the Law Courts now, I see how Asplund was dealing with exactly the same issues as we deal with everyday in our work; from the basic plan, the difficult elevation, down to the detail of the door handles. There is a good sense of continuity – he simply does it so much better.

Above: The main staircase leads to generous first floor circulation and waiting space as well as individual courtrooms.

Opposite: Central atrium at the Law Courts. The light and airy space sets the scene for a humane rather than authoritarian system of justice.

Courtyard elevation to the
Law Court extension building.
Extensive glazing ensures
plenty of natural light.

HOLDING COURT The Gothenburg Law Courts extension was the last major work by Erik Gunnar Asplund, widely regarded as the leading Swedish architect of the twentieth century. Asplund won a competition for it in 1913 and redesigned the scheme many times over the next twenty years. His 1913 design proposed to completely rework the original building, which dated from the seventeenth century, and reclad the facades in the then-in-vogue national romantic style. Various neo-classical revised designs followed before the project was shelved in 1925. When it was revived nine years later, Asplund was asked to retain the vocabulary of the original building on the main square elevation, but the city authorities eventually accepted his modern approach.

The final steel-framed design creates a courtyard between the old and new buildings with a glass wall forming the internal façade of the extension.

New Gothenburg Law Courts were built recently, leaving the Asplund building awaiting a new use.

Asplund's Law Courts are an extension (right) of an earlier building (left) and are entered through the original grand entrance and a courtyard.

William Mann (left) and Stephen Witherford (right) outside Utrecht City Hall. To the right the new wing incorporates a 'ruin' built from remnants of the building it replaced.

Utrecht City Hall

Location: Utrecht, Netherlands
Architect: Enric Miralles Benedetta Tagliabue Architects (EMBT)
Completed: 2000
Chosen by Stephen Witherford and William Mann of Witherford Watson Mann Architects.

Stephen Witherford

We first came to Utrecht City Hall in a spirit of enquiry rather than expectation – we were researching town halls for a competition shortly after we set up. It hadn't been extensively published and we were really taken aback. We were struck by the deft reworking of existing spaces, and inspired by the way the project renewed the institution by working with its past.

The city hall was an assemblage of houses at a bend in the Oudegracht canal, close to the ruined gothic cathedral. Although the city is growing, the council took the visionary decision to make the city hall smaller and more personal, moving some services to an administrative centre and leaving just the representative functions on the old site. It's good to see that the intended spirit of openness still holds: there's an intimate buzz about the place, and a welcoming spirit – and some of that is down to the architecture.

Miralles Tagliabue's project re-establishes the grain of the houses, their cross-walls and gardens twisting around the bend in the canal, making this institutional building both intimate and porous. The practice moved the entrance to the back away from the canal, demolished the 1930s wing, and extended the square towards the heart of the building. The grain of the houses flows out, forming a relaxed set of steps infilled with clinker bricks and stone. This informal approach means the entrance feels like a back door, in the best sense.

Alongside the new entrance the new wing is faced with a 'ruin', using pieces of the demolished 1930s building. On the lower levels, it's left as a stand-alone structure but the new building merges into it above. Other

architects might have left it as a fragment but Miralles never allows himself to leave it at the purely picturesque level.

The idea of the grain comes through particularly in the stair to the offices, which shows the invention, versatility and doggedness you need with existing buildings. The stair runs across the grain, so the walls it breaks through are left hanging and sticking out, and the treads alternate between wood, steel and concrete.

The council chamber works the civic and domestic scales very nicely: it combines four rooms over two levels into a single volume. The intermediate floor beams are left hanging, picked up where the cross-wall used to be by two large steel portals. So there's a sense of scale and openness but also of intimacy in this little amphitheatre.

The furnishing is very quirky and personal, and that's consistent with the themes in the building. This comes through in places such as the small wedding room where the benches are made from a variety of typical Dutch household chairs, the lights are deliberately mismatched, and there's a domestic dresser when you come in. This room was done by the artist Jurgen Bey, who used objects borrowed from the city museum to give a feeling of historical depth, but in a way you might find in someone's house. In the entrance foyer, the medieval hall is exposed over its full height and used as a collective memory wall hung with painted and photographic portraits of ordinary citizens as well as eminent ones.

The redesign de-institutionalises everything. It refuses to be a claustrophobic environment with generic corridors and spaces. Instead, there is abundant natural light from all angles and

directions throughout the generous communal spaces. Because it's a collage of structure, furniture, surfaces and artefacts, it doesn't get exhausting in the way that institutional buildings can. It's a joyful place to work.

It's quite a challenging building; almost overladen with ideas. But that spirit of restless enquiry is maybe why it's still alive for us. These issues of public space, historical depth, collective life keep confronting us in our work, and there aren't that many projects that address them with the seriousness and the confidence they deserve. This is definitely one of them.

William Mann

In *The Architecture of the City*, Aldo Rossi writes about the pathos of ruined houses, how they evoke 'the interrupted destiny of the individual...his often sad and difficult participation in the collective'.

At Utrecht City Hall, Miralles Tagliabue worked with ideas of house and ruin to break open a closed public building. But the spirit of ruin is exuberant and playful, it's not a mournful building at all. You can feel a living intelligence in every corner.

You certainly can't describe the project as restoration – it's more creative destruction. The core of the city hall had been wrapped in a classical skin in the nineteenth century, and its courtyard closed off by a 1930s block. Miralles Tagliabue took this closed arrangement and stable appearance, and tore it open, demolishing most of the thirties block, cutting into the classical 'wrap', carving the medieval hall at the heart of the building free from this

dignified but mismatched façade. A lot of the spaces work this tension between core and skin.

Miralles talked in an interview about traces of the past and his idea of time "as if instead of having it behind your back, you had it before you". I think he meant that by breaking open or scraping back, you can feel or see the depth of time beneath the present, rather than the past just being buried. I think we can learn from this attitude – but it's not for the faint-hearted.

Open figures – or ruins – run through the project, from strategy to detail. By demolishing the thirties block, the strategy turns a closed circuit, an 'O', into an open 'L' – a head (council chamber and medieval hall) with a long, twisted tail (offices). The details echo this: T-shaped beams, strips of plaster chiselled off to expose the brick, mats like shafts of light projected from doorways – nothing is self-contained, everything is incomplete, imperfect, interlocked.

The design sacrifices the strength of the new for the harmony of the whole. It's a way of working that takes a particular visual and constructional intelligence – there is no linear path between strategy and detail, they are more flexibly linked. The overall strategy has to adapt and distort to many local conditions, while still keeping its coherence. The project achieves this elusive aim very convincingly, because strategy and detail talk about the same things – openness, ruin, the domestic scale, homeliness. Every bit of the building has been thought about and loved. And how many of us, hand on heart, can really say that of our work?

It's all part of a vision that was shared between architect and client, to make local democracy personal. They call it their 'house of democracy'.

In a way the building combines the best of the Netherlands – its lively, open democracy – with the more Mediterranean sense of a civilisation built up bit by bit over time. Miralles Tagliabue's slow, rich sensibility is very suited to this complex assemblage in one of the oldest Dutch cities. It's a relatively rare example of international architecture effecting a kind of cultural exchange.

TOWN HALL REVIVAL Enric Miralles was appointed to 'rehabilitate' Utrecht town hall in 1997. The town hall was made up of ten conjoined medieval houses and halls, unified superficially by a nineteenth-century neoclassical facade and then further extended in the 1930s. Charged with making the town hall more open and inviting, Miralles chose interventions that made the older buildings more legible internally while radically re-orientating the site.

The 1930s registry extension at the rear was demolished and a new entrance created. New facilities for civil servants were built behind a 'ruin' that incorporates elements of the demolished building. The main hall, a medieval house, has been preserved in the heart of the building. The council chamber was redesigned to create an 8m-high space overlooked by the mayor's office. Miralles designed most of the furniture and light fittings as well as a water feature in the square.

Miralles died shortly before the completion of the building in 2000.

Above: The new entrance foyer abuts a medieval hall which is hung with portraits as a collective memory wall.

Opposite: View up through the extension. Architects EMBT created an "exuberant and playful" intervention that harmonised with the building's complex past.

Alex Mowat in front of
Santa Caterina Market,
which was regenerated
with an undulating new
roof over a retained
formal façade.

Santa Caterina Market

Location: Barcelona, Spain
Architect: Enric Miralles Benedetta Tagliabue (EMBT)
Completed: 1997–2005
Chosen by Alex Mowat of Mowat & Company

My first experience of Barcelona's Santa Caterina Market was accidental. At the time, the area was undergoing significant regeneration and I could see the nearly finished market through a gap in the hoardings. There was no one around, so it was easy to slip through and explore the building that I recognised from drawings in magazines.

The building consists of an exquisitely crafted and eccentric new roof flying over the walls of a neo-classical market built on a site formerly occupied by ecclesiastical buildings. EMBT exploited the poetry of this layering in the refurbishment, which retains the formal façade and central entrance while adding new elements that 'draw' in a different hand over the existing buildings.

The new roof is a fantastically engineered structure and gives three important aspects.

The first is a top layer made from coloured hexagonal ceramic tiles. Here EMBT picked up on the very Spanish tradition of ceramics, but used them on a much bigger scale and with a pattern that doesn't repeat. It's like a magic carpet floating over the activity below. Every apartment around the market gets a view of giant pixelated fruit and vegetables, including two big tomatoes and an aubergine. This extraordinary and unexpected image gives something back to the city.

Secondly, there is the view from the street, where the building keeps the parapet line of the original but with the new structure just meandering over the top. Sometimes the roof is supported on the inside of the old wall and sometimes on the outside by a series of twisted, tree-like columns that look like they don't belong in the city.

The structural geometry is non-repeating and feels very individual, handmade and low-tech. By never revealing all the structure from one viewpoint, frequently you're not too sure what's holding it up. These external views act as such a strong sign for the market that there is hardly any need for typographic signage.

The third view of the roof is from the inside. Here, the timbered underside bears no relation to the ceramic exuberance above but appears folded, with slashes of daylight coming in between the folds.

Visually and acoustically, the timber underside gives a texture and softness. This is very different to the harder, more formal painted ironwork structures of typical Spanish markets. Some of the timber is new and some made from the large old rafters of the previous building. Strangely, only one end of these rafters bears on masonry in the traditional way. The other end is suspended.

This combination of materials continues into the detailing at a lower level. Here it's not precious; it's been designed to wear in, rather than wear out, through the use of exposed brickwork and unvarnished timber. You can't really distinguish the new timbers from the old timbers.

Where the white render of the neo-classical walls meets the pavement, the render has been cut away to reveal the brickwork. The more bashed it gets by cars, roadsweepers and rain, the better it gets. No one will be jet-washing the stonework here.

The materiality of each elevation is subtly different. When the surrounding streets get narrower, the walls get rougher.

The south wall is rather strange. The patterning is wilful: rough stone is overlaid with smooth marble panels that appear to be the remains of old water troughs. Integral water fountains for thirsty passers-by animate the wall.

This project is inspiring not just for its integration of old and new materials, textures and forms but for its coherent mix of different uses – including the provision of social housing, that places sheltered homes for the elderly above the market and right in the heart of the city. This is a practical location for elderly housing and the opposite of the conventional UK suburban model.

It's also pioneering in its integration of technology to assist the mix of uses and resident life. There is a digital ordering system for the stall owners and also a subterranean organic-waste processing plant for the wider neighbourhood. Hatches in the market wall connect to waste chutes.

There's something very inspiring about mixing retail with other uses and giving retail such a civic quality as EMBT did at Santa Caterina. The tradition of covered markets and elegant arcades is so long lost in Britain that we often don't even realise this typology has gone.

Santa Caterina is very much the centrepiece of this dense urban neighbourhood. It intervenes in the city grain to contribute a different amenity to the area by creating, in the refurbishment, two new public spaces that are unlike the regular streets of Barcelona's grid. The one at the north is very flat, formal and civic; in the second, at the south-east corner, the architects carved out something much smaller, more informal and asymmetric. The informality is further emphasised by the

steep camber, which rises up and over the archaeological remains below.

The interior space still has a very public character, and that's a difficult thing to achieve. The interior has the same generosity of interior and permeability as the Royal Festival Hall. There is no formal way of using the building; you just meander through.

I don't think this project, despite its roof and place-specific materials, should be seen as just a bit of flamboyant Catalan colour. There's no reason why this couldn't work elsewhere.

Santa Caterina is both civilised and civic, balancing so many priorities: commerce, elderly housing, rubbish, as well as archaeological remains. The combinations of new and old building fabric, logical, simple design and extraordinarily wilful elements, the mix of uses, traditional market retail and new technology are something we can all learn from in making our cities.

Coming back after five years, the market is worn in and relaxed, as if people have learned how to use it and love it. It's very egalitarian – a nice building to have in your neighbourhood.

I understand Benedetta Tagliabue lives locally and is a regular shopper. To share a space that you have designed, and which is cleary loved by those in your neighbourhood, must be a great reward for any architect: something to aspire to, and to be inspired by.

Twisted, tree-like columns support the new roof structure. The market regeneration was part of a wider project involving new housing for the elderly on an adjacent site.

Inside the market, the timber underside of the new roof is a muted contrast to its colourful exterior cladding, designed to resemble pixelated fruit and vegetables.

MARKET REVAMP Santa Caterina Market in Barcelona's historic quarter dated from 1844–8 and was badly in need of regeneration when EMBT took on the job in 1997. The brief was not just to revive the market but to incorporate social housing, a small museum and an underground car park.

The scheme also incorporates a waste processing centre, and creates two small public spaces. The project was extensively delayed with the result that, although the design predated the Scottish Parliament, it was completed after that building was finished – and after the death of Miralles. The delay was due to a series of archaeological finds during construction, which included the remains of a Dominican monastery, a thirteenth-century gothic church, and the ruins of a Roman necropolis.

EMBT's design retained just the market's façade and introduced a wave-like roof of 325,000 ceramic tiles supported on intertwining steel columns.

Picture credits and acknowledgements

Pamela Buxton is a freelance architecture and design journalist. She has written for many specialist publications including *Building Design*, *RIBA Journal*, *Blueprint* and *Grand Designs* magazine.

Gareth Gardner is a London-based architectural photographer and writer. He takes photographs for many of the UK's leading architecture and interior design practices as well as pursuing personal projects. www.garethgardner.com

Edward Tyler is a professional photographer specialising in portraiture and architecture. He has exhibited in the National Portrait Gallery, and is married with two camera-shy sons. www.edtyler.com

This book brings together a selection of articles on twentieth century buildings first published in the architecture newspaper *Building Design* as part of its Inspiration series, which ran in print from 2009–2014 and has since continued online. Our thanks go to former Building Design editors Amanda Baillieu (who instigated the series) and Ellis Woodman, current editor Thomas Lane, and Building Design publisher UBM Built Environment.

The articles were only possible thanks to the enthusiastic participation of the nominating architects, who were generous with their time and thoughts when *Building Design* took them back to revisit the inspirational buildings that they had chosen. We were accompanied by one of the two principal photographers on the series, Gareth Gardner and Edward Tyler, who were responsible (with a few exceptions) for the evocative images in this book.

We would also like to thank all the building owners and occupants for allowing us to visit, and everyone else who helped make the visits, and the Inspiration series, such a success. Many apologies if anyone has been inadvertently omitted from the following list:

Workplace Stiftung Zollverein; Economist Group; Parti Communiste Français; Schlumberger; Erco.

Education Glasgow School of Art; Cranbrook Academy of Art; University of Leicester Engineering Faculty; Trinity College Dublin; St Catherine's College, Oxford; St John's College, Cambridge; Faculty of Architecture University of Porto; Hellerup School.

Cultural Buildings Fundació Mies van der Rohe; Maison de Verre; Museum Boijmans van Beuningen; Museo Civico di Castelvecchio; Liverpool Playhouse; Sainsbury Centre for the Visual Arts; Kunsthal Rotterdam; Palais de Tokyo.

Individual Houses National Trust; Cap Moderne; Kunstmuseen Krefeld; Fondo Ambiente Italiano; Maison Louis Carré; Axel Bruchhäuser.

Housing Developments Tautes Heim (www.tautes-heim.de); Corporation of London; Byker Community Trust.

Places of Worship Otto Wagner Spital; Grundtvigs Kirke; Notre Dame Du Haut; Metropolitan Cathedral of Christ the King, Liverpool.

Public Buildings Save Lucy Committee Inc.; Loos Bar; Skogskyrkogården; Landgoed Zonnestraal; Higab; Utrecht City Hall; EMBT; Mercat Santa Caterina.

Gareth Gardner
Cover image.
The Architects: p8 Cany Ash; Jonathan Ellis-Miller; Alex Ely; Tony Fretton; p9 Tom Grieve and Hana Loftus; Graham Howarth; Simon Hudspith; Edward Jones; p10 Alex Mowat; Eric Parry; Greg Penoyre; RCKa; Tim Ronalds; p11 Michael Squire; Marie-José van Hee; Jonathan Woolf.
Workplace: pp12-13; 14-19; 20-23; 24-29; 36-39; 40-43.
Education: pp76-69.
Cultural Buildings: pp78-79; 102-105.
Individual Houses: pp108-113; 116-119; 128-133.
Housing Developments: pp140-143; 144-149.
Places of Worship: pp186-191.
Public Buildings: pp212-217; 222-227; 232-235.

Edward Tyler
The Architects: p8 David Archer; Peter Barber; Rab and Denise Bennetts; Michál Cohen; Ted Cullinan; Biba Dow and Alun Jones; Sarah Featherstone; p9 Edgar Gonzalez; Piers Gough; Sean Griffiths; Russell Brown and Roger Hawkins; Stephen Hodder; Adam Khan; David Kohn; Julian Lewis; p10 MJ Long; Gerard Maccreanor; Niall McLaughlin; Paul Monaghan; Peter St John; Dominic Cullinan and Jon Buck; Takero Shimazaki; James Soane. p11 Studio Egret West; Hans van der Heijden; Paul Williams; Stephen Witherford and William Mann, Clare Wright.
Workplace: pp4-5, 30-35; 46-51; 44-45.
Education: pp44-45; 54-57; 58-61; 62-65; 66-69; 70-73; 74-77.
Cultural Buildings: pp82-85; 86-91; 92-93; 94-97; 98-100.

Individual Houses: pp106-107, 122-125; 134-137.
Housing Developments: pp150-153; 154-157; 158-161; 162-165; pp138-139, 166-169; 170-175; 176-179.
Places of Worship: pp180-185; 192-197; 200-203.
Public Buildings: pp204-205; 208-211; 218-221; 228-231.

Valerie Bennett p8 Tom Coward
Manuel Bougot/ADAGP, Paris 2015 pp114-115
James Cameron p10 Keith Williams
John East p120,198-199
Laura Evans p10 Patrick Lynch
Benedict Johnson p10 Richard Rogers
Olsen Studio p52
Save Lucy Committee, Inc p206
Pepo Segura – Fundació Mies van der Rohe pp80-81
Amelia Stein p10 John Tuomey

Index

238